THE SIEGE OF THE PEKING EMBASSY, 1900

uncovered editions

Series editor: Tim Coates

Other titles in the series

uncovered editions

THE SIEGE OF THE PEKING EMBASSY, 1900

SIR CLAUDE MACDONALD'S REPORT

ON THE BOXER REBELLION

∘◦⊰❈⊱◦∘

London: The Stationery Office

© The Stationery Office 2000

Applications for reproduction should be made in writing to
The Stationery Office Limited, St Crispins, Duke Street,
Norwich NR3 1PD.

ISBN 0 11 702456 2

First published as Cd 257, 1900 and Cd 442, April 1901
© Crown copyright

A CIP catalogue record for this book is available from the
British Library.

Typeset by J&L Composition Ltd, Filey, North Yorkshire.

Printed in the United Kingdom for The Stationery Office by
Biddles Ltd, Guildford, Surrey.
TJ1047   C30   09/00

Series editor: Tim Coates

Tim Coates studied at University College, Oxford and at the University of Stirling. After working in the theatre for a number of years, he took up bookselling and became managing director, firstly of Sherratt and Hughes bookshops, and then of Waterstone's. He is known for his support for foreign literature, particularly from the Czech Republic. The idea for 'Uncovered Editions' came while searching through the bookshelves of his late father-in-law, Air Commodore Patrick Cave OBE. He is married to Bridget Cave, has two sons, and lives in London.

Tim Coates welcomes views and ideas on the Uncovered Editions series. He can be e-mailed at timcoatesbooks@yahoo.com

The Boxer movement in China was a secret society which preached hatred of foreigners. By the spring of 1900, this movement was out of control. On 9 June, the Boxers launched their first attack against foreign property in Peking by burning down the racecourse. Sir Claude MacDonald, the British ambassador in Peking, lost no time in responding, and wired for a relief force to be sent from the port of Taku.

These are the diplomatic papers relating to the events during that turbulent period. In order to rescue the hundreds of diplomats and their families who were stranded inside the Legation buildings, the largest international force ever assembled in history fought its way from Taku to Peking. How they fared is described in the despatches. The central part of the story, however, is the gripping diary kept by Sir Claude MacDonald.

It may help the reader to be aware of this incident in two contexts. At the turn of the century the British Army and the diplomatic service were engaged in several conflicts round the world. The use of the telegraph to maintain contact with the highest authorities in the Government is evident throughout the siege, although the telegraph wires to the Legation Quarter were cut soon into the siege. The various consular staff in the region reported directly to the

Prime Minister, Lord Salisbury, who was dealing with this matter personally, and effectively, as he was with several other major matters at the same time.

The other aspect of this conflict that may assist the reader is a wider understanding of the relationship between China and the Western Powers during the preceding century. The approach had been to lend money and missionaries in an attempt develop a European style of civilisation and a capitalist industrial society with its infrastructure, particularly in the form of railways. It was the same approach as had been used in Africa. Debts to foreign countries became impossible to pay, and effectively led to the forfeit of a number of coastal cities to various countries. Thus Britain acquired Hong Kong, Shanghae and Wei-hai Weh, and there were towns which were leased to or protected by the Germans, the Russians and the French.

It was against this loss of their own historic civilisation and the moral and financial domination that was such a powerful force in their country, that the Boxer movement rose with tremendous violence. In this light the behaviour of the Dowager Empress might indeed be seen as heroic.

PART ONE

∞∞✕∞∞

CORRESPONDENCE CONCERNING THE
BOXER REBELLION IN CHINA

1900

Seymour's Advance, 1900

Sir C. MacDonald to the Marquess of Salisbury

(Telegraphic) *Peking, June* 4, 1900

I am informed by a Chinese courier who arrived to-day from Yung-Ching, 40 miles south of Peking, that on the 1st June the Church of England Mission at that place was attacked by the Boxers. He states that one missionary, Mr Robinson, was murdered, and that he saw his body, and that another, Mr Norman, was carried off by the Boxers. I am insisting on the Chinese authorities taking immediate measures to effect his rescue.

Sir E. Monson to the Marquess of Salisbury
(*received June* 4)

(Telegraphic)   *Paris, June* 4, 1900

The French Minister at Peking has informed the Minister for Foreign Affairs that the situation has, in his opinion, improved.

Sir C. MacDonald to the Marquess of Salisbury
(*received June* 5)

(Telegraphic)   *Peking, June* 4, 1900

Present situation at Peking is such that we may at any time be besieged here with the railway and telegraph lines cut. In the event of this occurring, I beg your Lordship will cause urgent instructions to be sent to Admiral Seymour to consult with the officers commanding the other foreign squadrons now at Taku to take concerted measures for our relief.

The above was agreed to at a meeting held to-day by the foreign Representatives, and a similar telegram was sent to their respective Governments by the Ministers of Austria, Italy, Germany, France, Japan, Russia, and the United States, all of whom have ships at Taku and guards here.

The telegram was proposed by the French Minister and carried unanimously. It is difficult to say whether the situation is as grave as the latter supposes, but the apathy of the Chinese Government makes it very serious.

Admiralty to Foreign Office (received June 5)

Sir,   June 5, 1900

I am commanded by my Lords Commissioners of the Admiralty to transmit, for the information of the Secretary of State for Foreign Affairs, a copy of a telegram, dated 4th June, from the Commander-in-chief, China.

EVAN MACGREGOR

Enclosure

Vice-Admiral Sir E. Seymour to Admiralty

(Telegraphic)   *Tong-ku, June 4, 1900*

"D'Entrecasteaux" (French), "Kasagi" (Japanese), "Zenta" (Austrian), arrived. Twenty-four men-of-war here altogether.

A guard of 75 sent to Peking and 104 to Tien-tsin, matters being reported serious. I remain awaiting developments and further news from Minister.

Sir C. MacDonald to the Marquess of Salisbury
(received June 5)

(Telegraphic)   *Peking, June 5, 1900*

My telegram of yesterday.

I went this afternoon to the Yamên★ to inquire of the Ministers personally what steps the Chinese Government proposed to take to effect the punishment of Mr Robinson's murderers and the release of Mr Norman.

I was informed by the Ministers that the Viceroy was the responsible person, that they had telegraphed

★ Office or residence of a Chinese public official.

to him to send troops to the spot, and that that was all they were able to do in the matter.

They did not express regret or show the least anxiety to effect the relief of the imprisoned man, and they displayed the greatest indifference during the interview. I informed them that the Chinese Government would be held responsible by Her Majesty's Government for the criminal apathy which had brought about this disgraceful state of affairs. I then demanded an interview with Prince Ching, which is fixed for to-morrow, as I found it useless to discuss the matter with the Yamên.

Sir C. MacDonald to the Marquess of Salisbury
(received June 5)

(Telegraphic)   *Peking, June* 5, 1900

My preceding telegram.

I regret to say I have received confirmation of the reported murder of Mr Robinson. Her Majesty's Consul at Tien-tsin has been informed by the Viceroy of the murder on 2nd June of Mr Norman, who was supposed to be a prisoner.

Consul Carles to the Marquess of Salisbury
(received June 5)

(Telegraphic)   *Tien-tsin, June* 5, 1900

Urgent. I have to-day sent the following telegram to the Admiral:

"At a meeting of the Consuls held yesterday to form a home guard, a Resolution was passed asking for strong reinforcements. This step I consider to be absolutely necessary. Our passive position intensifies the danger of the situation hour by hour, and I strongly urge the advisability of the guard being permitted to take active measures of hostility.

"I am telegraphing to Her Majesty's Minister, but am doubtful how long communications may remain open with Peking."

Sir E. Monson to the Marquess of Salisbury
(received June 6)

(Extract)   *Paris, June* 5, 1900

I asked M. Delcassé last evening what news he had from Peking, observing that the telegrams published in the French papers as to the dangerous situation in that capital were confirmed, as far as I knew, by the information sent to your Lordship by Her Majesty's Minister.

M. Delcassé replied that, on the contrary, his latest telegrams from M. Pichon represented that he considered that for the moment all imminent danger was over.

M. Delcassé could not tell me the date of M. Pichon's telegram, but his Excellency seemed to be convinced that it was subsequent to anything that had appeared in the newspapers, and to believe that all the Europeans at first reported missing had escaped.

Sir C. MacDonald to the Marquess of Salisbury
(received June 6)

(Telegraphic)   *Peking, June* 5, 1900

As the wire to Tien-tsin may be cut at any moment, please send immediate instructions to the Admiral.

Sir C. MacDonald to the Marquess of Salisbury
(received June 6)

(Telegraphic)   *Peking, June* 5, 1900

This afternoon I had an interview with the Prince and Ministers of the Yamên. They expressed much regret at the murder of Messrs Robinson and Norman, and their tone was fully satisfactory in this respect.

I pointed out that there was not the slightest indication that the Chinese Government intended to deal severely with the Boxer disturbances, and that insecurity of human life within a few miles of the capital and serious danger of an outbreak occurring within the city itself was the result of this attitude.

I said that this failure to suppress the Boxers was, as far as I could judge, leading straight to foreign intervention, however much friendly Powers might regret such a course.

No attempt was made by the Prince to defend the Chinese Government, nor to deny what I had said. He could say nothing to reassure me as to the safety of the city, and admitted that the Government was reluctant to deal harshly with the movement, which, owing to its anti-foreign character, was popular. He stated that they were bringing 6,000 soldiers from near Tien-tsin for the protection of the railway, but it was evident that he doubted whether they would be allowed to fire on the Boxers except in the defence of Government property, or if authorized whether they would obey.

He gave me to understand, without saying so directly, that he has entirely failed to induce the

Court to accept his own views as to the danger of inaction. It was clear, in fact, that the Yamên wished me to understand that the situation was most serious, and that, owing to the influence of ignorant advisers with the Empress-Dowager, they were powerless to remedy it.

Sir C. MacDonald to the Marquess of Salisbury
(received June 6)

(Telegraphic)   *Peking, June 6, 1900*

Since the interview with the Yamên reported in my preceding telegram I have seen several of my colleagues.

I find they all agree that, owing to the now evident sympathy of the Empress-Dowager and the more conservative of her advisers with the anti-foreign movement, the situation is rapidly growing more serious.

Should there be no change in the attitude of the Empress, a rising in the city, ending in anarchy, which may produce rebellion in the provinces, will be the result, "failing an armed occupation of Peking by one or more of the Powers."

Our ordinary means of pressure on the Chinese Government fail, as the Yamên is by general consent, and their own admission, powerless to persuade the Court to take serious measures of repression. Direct representations to the Emperor and Dowager-Empress from the Corps Diplomatique at a special audience seems to be the only remaining chance of impressing the Court.

At to-day's meeting of the foreign Representatives, it will probably be decided to ask the approval of their respective Governments for the demand for such an audience, unless it appears that the situation is so critical as to justify them in making it without waiting for instructions.

As no foreign Representative here has Ambassador's privileges it is probable that an audience will be refused, as against precedent, and it is certain to be delayed should the demand be refused, or unless there is an improvement in the situation (as there may be if the demand itself opens the Empress's eyes).

I am of opinion that strong measures should be taken to enforce compliance.

Sir C. MacDonald to the Marquess of Salisbury
(received June 6)

(Telegraphic)   *Peking, June* 6, 1900

My preceding telegram.

A meeting of the foreign Representatives was held this afternoon, and it was decided to postpone till Saturday next the question of demanding an audience.

Admiralty to Foreign Office (received June 6)

Sir,   *June* 6, 1900

I am commanded by my Lords Commissioners of the Admiralty to transmit, for the information of the Secretary of State for Foreign Affairs, a copy of a telegram, dated this day, from the Commander-in-chief, China.

EVAN MACGREGOR

Enclosure

Vice-Admiral Sir E. Seymour to Admiralty

(Telegraphic) *Tong-ku, June 6, 1900*

Situation having become more grave, I have ordered "Aurora" and "Phœnix" here from Wei-hai Wei; "Humber" to Shanhaikuan. Several Europeans in isolated positions have been murdered, and there is a strong feeling against all foreign element. Chinese Government appear to be doing nothing to check outrages. Meeting of Senior Naval Officers of the French, German, Italian, Russian, Austrian, United States, and Japanese men-of-war held on board "Centurion" this afternoon to discuss situation and arrange concerted action if necessary.

Admiralty to Foreign Office (received June 6)

Sir, *June 6, 1900*

I am commanded by my Lords Commissioners of the Admiralty to transmit, for the information of the Secretary of State for Foreign Affairs, a copy of a telegram, dated this day, to the Commander-in-chief, China.

EVAN MACGREGOR

Enclosure

Admiralty to Vice-Admiral Sir E. Seymour

(Telegraphic) *June 6, 1900*

In case of danger to the foreign Legations at Peking, or to British subjects either there or at Tien-tsin and in the neighbourhood, take such steps, in concert with the Commanding Officers of the other squadrons, as you may consider advisable and practicable for their protection. Her Majesty's Government desire to leave you a wide discretion as to the measures to be adopted.

Foreign Office to Admiralty

Sir,   *June* 6, 1900

Her Majesty's Minister in China, in his telegram of the 4th instant, of which a copy was communicated to you yesterday, stated that the situation at Peking was such that Her Majesty's Legation might at any time be besieged, with the railway and telegraph lines cut. He requested that in the event of this happening, urgent instructions might be sent to the Commander-in-chief on the China station to consult with the officers in command of the squadrons of other Powers at Taku, with a view to concerted measures for the relief of the foreign Legations at Peking. Sir C. MacDonald added that his telegram was the result of a decision arrived at at a meeting of the foreign Representatives, and that similar telegrams had been sent by the Ministers of Austria–Hungary, Italy, Germany, France, Japan, Russia, and the United States to their respective Governments, all of whom have guards at Peking and ships at Taku.

In a further telegram received to-day, of which a copy has also been transmitted to you, Sir C. MacDonald states that the telegraph to Tien-tsin may be interrupted at any moment, and repeats his request that the instructions suggested in his first telegram may be sent to Admiral Seymour.

The Marquess of Salisbury would suggest that the Lords Commissioners of the Admiralty should telegraph to the Commander-in-chief in China, that, in case of danger to the foreign Legations at Peking or to British subjects either there or at Tien-tsin and in the neighbourhood, he should take such steps in concert with the Commanding Officers of the other squadrons as he may consider advisable and practicable for their protection; and that Her Majesty's Government desire to leave him a wide discretion as to the measures which, under the circumstances, it may appear to him expedient to adopt.

FRANCIS BERTIE

Admiralty to Foreign Office (received June 7)

Sir,   *June* 7, 1900

I am commanded by my Lords Commissioners of the Admiralty to transmit, for the information of the Secretary of State for Foreign Affairs, a copy of a telegram, dated the 7th June, from the Commander-in-chief, China station.

A copy of this telegram has been sent to the Colonial Office and also to the War Office.

EVAN MACGREGOR

Enclosure

Vice-Admiral Sir E. Seymour to Admiralty

(Telegraphic)   *Tong-ku, June* 7, 1900

In view of the gravity of the situation, and it being unadvisable to distress ships for men, submit whether troops from Hong Kong may be sent for Tien-tsin and Peking. "Terrible" available for conveyance.

Admiralty to Foreign Office (received June 7)

Sir,   *June* 7, 1900

I am commanded by my Lords Commissioners of the Admiralty to transmit, for the information of the Secretary of State for Foreign Affairs, a copy of a telegram, dated the 7th instant, from Admiralty to the Commander-in-chief, China.

EVAN MACGREGOR

Enclosure

Admiralty to Vice-Admiral Sir E. Seymour

(Telegraphic)   *June* 7, 1900

Following telegram has been addressed by Secretary of State for Foreign Affairs to Her Majesty's Minister, Peking:

"The situation is difficult, and your discretion must be quite unfettered. You may take precisely what measures you think expedient."

Report any steps you may take in concert with Minister.

The Marquess of Salisbury to Sir C. MacDonald

(Telegraphic)   *Foreign Office, June* 7, 1900

With reference to your telegram of the 5th instant, I have to inform you that the following instructions were telegraphed yesterday to the Admiral:

[*See Enclosure in Evan MacGregor's despatch to Foreign Office, dated June 6 1900*]

The Marquess of Salisbury to Sir C. MacDonald
(Telegraphic)   *Foreign Office, June* 7, 1900
Your telegram of the 6th June.
The situation is difficult, and your discretion must be quite unfettered. You may take precisely what measures you think expedient.

The Marquess of Salisbury to Sir C. MacDonald
(Telegraphic)   *Foreign Office, June* 7, 1900
With reference to your telegram of the 6th June on the subject of the crisis at Peking, I approve the proposal to demand an audience of the Emperor and Empress-Dowager.

Sir C. MacDonald to the Marquess of Salisbury
(Telegraphic)   *Peking, June* 7, 1900
There is a long Decree in the "Gazette" which ascribes the recent trouble to the favour shown to converts in law suits and the admission to their ranks of bad characters. It states that the Boxers, who are the objects of the Throne's sympathy equally with the converts, have made use of the anti-Christian feeling aroused by these causes, and that bad characters among them have destroyed chapels and railways which are the property of the State.

Unless the ringleaders among such bad characters are now surrendered by the Boxers they will be dealt with as disloyal subjects, and will be exterminated. Authorization will be given to the Generals to effect arrests, exercising discrimination between leaders and their followers.

It is probable that the above Decree represents a compromise between the conflicting opinions which exist at Court. The general tone is most unsatisfactory, though the effect may be good if severe measures are actually taken. The general lenient tone, the absence of reference to the murder of missionaries, and the justification of the proceedings of the Boxers by the misconduct of Christian converts are all dangerous factors in the case.

Admiralty to Foreign Office (received June 8)

Sir,   *June* 8, 1900
With reference to previous correspondence, I am commanded by my Lords Commissioners of the Admiralty to transmit, for the information of the Secretary of State for Foreign Affairs, a copy of a telegram of the 8th June from the Commander-in-chief on the China station relative to affairs at Peking.

EVAN MACGREGOR

Enclosure

Vice-Admiral Sir E. Seymour to Admiralty

(Telegraphic)   *Tong-ku, June* 8, 1900
My telegram of 6th instant.

In case of a sudden march on Peking as regards command, the best course might be for me to undertake it, with Russian Colonel as Chief of the Staff. I think all or most of the foreign officers here would agree to this. Request instructions.

Rear-Admiral would be left in the command of the squadron off Pei-ho.

Admiralty to Foreign Office (received June 8)

Sir,   June 8, 1900

I am commanded by my Lords Commissioners of the Admiralty to transmit, for the information of the Secretary of State for Foreign Affairs, a copy of a telegram, dated this day, from the Admiralty to the Commander-in-chief on the China station.

A similar communication has been addressed to the War Office.

EVAN MACGREGOR

Enclosure

Admiralty to Vice-Admiral Sir E. Seymour

(Telegraphic)   June 8, 1900

With reference to your telegram of the 7th instant, you are to place yourself in communication with the General Commanding at Hong Kong, and concert with him as to dispatch of any troops from there to the Pei-ho should it be considered desirable.

The Marquess of Salisbury to Sir C. MacDonald

(Telegraphic)   *Foreign Office, June 8, 1900*

I have been informed by the Spanish Government that, having no guard to send to protect their Legation at Peking, they would be glad if the British force could undertake that duty.

If the British force is sufficiently strong, you can comply with any application from your Spanish colleague to this effect.

Foreign Office to Admiralty

Sir,   *June* 8, 1900

With reference to the inquiry of the Commander-in-chief on the China station as to who should be in command of the force from the foreign ships of war in the event of a march on Peking becoming necessary, I am to state that, in Lord Salisbury's opinion, the Senior Officer should command the force, and Sir Edward Seymour should be so informed.

FRANCIS BERTIE

Foreign Office to Admiralty

Sir,   *June* 8, 1900

I have laid before the Marquess of Salisbury your letter of to-day, enclosing a copy of a telegram from the Commander-in-chief on the China station, in which he proposes that, in the event of it being necessary for the forces from the foreign ships of war to march to Peking, he should take command of them, with the Russian Colonel as Chief of his Staff.

Lord Salisbury suggests that Admiral Seymour's proposal should be approved.

FRANCIS BERTIE

Foreign Office to War Office

Sir,   *June* 8, 1900

The Lords Commissioners of the Admiralty have communicated to the Marquess of Salisbury a copy of a telegram from the Commander-in-chief on the China station of yesterday, in which he suggests that, in view of the gravity of the situation in Northern China, and the inadvisability of leaving Her Majesty's ships without sufficient crews, troops should be sent from Hong Kong for employment at Tien-tsin and Peking.

A copy of Admiral Seymour's telegram has been sent to Her Majesty's Secretary of State for War.

I am directed by Lord Salisbury to state that he considers it advisable that all the troops that can be spared, not only from Hong Kong, but also from Wei-hai Wei and Singapore, should be concentrated at Taku.

His Lordship would be glad to be informed what steps Lord Lansdowne proposes to take in the matter after communicating with the Lords Commissioners of the Admiralty.

FRANCIS BERTIE

Sir C. MacDonald to the Marquess of Salisbury
(received June 9)

(Telegraphic)   *Peking, June* 8, 1900

A very bad effect has been produced by the Decree reported in my immediately preceding telegram. There is no prohibition of the Boxers drilling, which they now openly do in the houses of the Manchu nobility and in the temples. This Legation is full of British refugees, mostly women and children, and the London and Church of England Missions have been abandoned.

I trust that the instructions requested in my telegrams of the 4th and 5th instant have been sent to the Admiral.

Sir C. MacDonald to the Marquess of Salisbury
(received June 9)

(Telegraphic)   *Peking, June* 8, 1900

I have received the following telegram, dated noon to-day, from Her Majesty's Consul at Tien-tsin:

"By now the Boxers must be near Yang-tsun. Last night the bridge, which is outside that station, was seen to be on fire. General Nieh's forces are being withdrawn to Lutai, and 1,500 of them have already passed through by railway. There are now at Yang-tsun an engine and trucks ready to take 2,000 more men."

Lutai lies on the other side of Tien-tsin, and at some distance. Should this information be correct, it means that an attempt to protect Peking has been abandoned by the only force on which the Yamên profess to place any reliance.

The 6,000 men mentioned in my telegram of the 5th instant were commanded by General Nieh.

Sir C. MacDonald to the Marquess of Salisbury
(received June 9)

(Telegraphic) *Peking, June 8, 1900*

I have sent the following telegram to-day to Tôkiô:

"I have been instructed by Lord Salisbury to inform you of the present position here by telegraph.

"The movement against foreigners—has been permitted to develop until it has resulted in the burning of railway stations, the interruption for the last five days of communication by rail, the murder in the country, near Peking, of two British missionaries and several foreigners, and in the surrounding districts the destruction of chapels and the pillage of numerous converts. In Peking itself British missionaries have been forced to quit their houses and come for refuge to the Legation, which has a guard of marines for its protection.

"The Chinese Government have been so far moved by these events as to depute high officials to hold parley with the 'Boxers,' but give no indication of any intention to suppress them summarily. Probably they still have the power to do so, but sympathy with the movement strongly influences the Throne, and the temper of the troops is uncertain.

"There is a disposition on the part of the Diplomatic Corps to request an audience, in order to represent the seriousness of the situation to the Throne, but as yet I am not aware whether this step will meet with the approval of Her Majesty's Government."

Sir C. MacDonald to the Marquess of Salisbury
(received June 9)

(Telegraphic)   *Peking, June* 8, 1900

With reference to my telegrams of the 5th and 6th instant and my two immediately preceding telegrams, I have to report that the situation is now critical. To-morrow or next day we shall meet to decide the question of a personal audience with the Empress-Dowager and the Emperor. If the demand for an audience is made it is essential, first, that it should be insisted on, and that we should compel the Chinese Government to grant it; secondly, that a definite statement should be made to the Throne, when the audience takes place, putting in plain terms the existence of so deplorable a state of things in North China owing to the Boxers not being repressed, and concluding with a strong intimation that, unless the Chinese Government immediately suppressed the Boxers and re-established law and order, the foreign Powers would be compelled themselves to take measures to that end, as the present state of things is fraught with so much danger to foreign interests.

Admiralty to Foreign Office (received June 9)

Sir,   *June* 8, 1900

I am commanded by my Lords Commissioners of the Admiralty to transmit, for the information of the Secretary of State for Foreign Affairs, copy of a telegram, dated the 8th June, from Admiralty to Commander-in-chief, China, with reference to your letter of to-day, concerning Admiral Seymour's proposal as to the command of any forces sent to Peking.

EVAN MACGREGOR

Enclosure
Admiralty to Vice-Admiral Sir E. Seymour

(Telegraphic) *June* 8, 1900

Yours of the 8th instant.

Your proposal is approved if agreement come to.

Admiralty to Foreign Office (received June 9)

Sir, *June* 9, 1900

I am commanded by my Lords Commissioners of the Admiralty to transmit, for the information of the Secretary of State for Foreign Affairs, a copy of a telegram, dated to-day, from Admiralty to the Commander-in-chief, China.

A copy has also been sent to the War Office.

EVAN MACGREGOR

Enclosure
Admiralty to Vice-Admiral Sir E. Seymour

(Telegraphic) *June* 9, 1900

With reference to Admiralty telegram of yesterday, War Office has authorized Hong Kong and Straits Settlements to give such military force as they can spare on your request, should they be required.

War Office to Foreign Office (received June 9)

Sir,   *June 9, 1900*

I am directed by the Secretary of State for War to acknowledge the receipt of Foreign Office letter of 8th June relative to the situation in China.

In reply, I am to acquaint you, for the information of the Marquess of Salisbury, that the Admiralty has informed the Admiral on the station that the General Officers in command at Hong Kong and Singapore have been instructed to meet any demand for troops that he may make upon them to the extent that they can be spared.

The General Officers concerned have been instructed to comply as far as possible with the demands of the Admiral.

R. H. KNOX

The Marquess of Salisbury to Sir C. MacDonald

(Telegraphic)   *Foreign Office, June 9, 1900*

The Admiral has pointed out the inadvisability of unduly depleting the ships of war.

In consequence of his representation he has been informed that, in the event of his requiring them, troops from Hong Kong and Singapore will be placed at his disposal.

The Marquess of Salisbury to Sir C. MacDonald

(Telegraphic)   *Foreign Office, June 9, 1900*

I concur in the proposal contained in your telegram of yesterday with regard to the intimation to be made to the Emperor and Dowager-Empress at the audience it is proposed to demand.

Foreign Office to Admiralty

Sir,   *June* 9, 1900

I am directed by the Marquess of Salisbury to inform you that the Spanish Government, having no guard to send to Peking to protect their Legation there, have requested that that duty may be undertaken by the British force.

I enclose, for the information of the Lords Commissioners of the Admiralty, a copy of a telegram which Lord Salisbury has sent to Her Majesty's Minister in China [dated June 8 1900] instructing him to comply with any application to the above effect from his Spanish colleague, if the British force is sufficient.

FRANCIS BERTIE

Admiralty to Foreign Office (*received June* 10)

Sir,   *June* 10, 1900

I am commanded by my Lords Commissioners of the Admiralty to transmit, for the information of the Secretary of State for Foreign Affairs, copy of a telegram, dated the 10th June, from the Commander-in-chief, China station, reporting his landing for advance to Peking.

EVAN MACGREGOR

Enclosure

Vice-Admiral Sir E. Seymour to Admiralty

(Telegraphic)   *Tong-ku, June* 10, 1900

Following telegram received from Minister at Peking:

"Situation extremely grave. Unless arrangements are made for immediate advance to Peking it will be too late."

In consequence of above, I am landing at once with all available men, and have asked foreign officers' co-operation.

Consul Carles to the Marquess of Salisbury
(received June 10)

(Telegraphic)   *Tien-tsin, June* 10, 1900

At my request a meeting of Consuls and Naval Commandants was held last night to consider the urgent request of Her Majesty's Minister for the immediate arrangement for the dispatch to Peking of guards.

The Japanese, Italians, Austrians, and Americans agreed to join with us in dispatching all men available as guards for the protection of the working party which is restoring the railway and for the gradual advance for the relief of the Legations, which was to take place as the line was repaired.

The French and Russians refused to dispatch guards unless a force of at least 1,500 men was sent or the line was in working order. It was suggested that this or larger force could, if the situation was really as grave as was painted, be asked for from Port Arthur. It was agreed between us to ask the Viceroy to furnish a train, and the detachments will leave this morning, if possible, without awaiting the Russians and French.

Consul Carles to the Marquess of Salisbury
(*received June* 10)

(Telegraphic)   *Tien-tsin, June* 10, 1900
The Commander-in-chief on the China station, with 300 British, 100 Americans, 60 Austrians, and 40 Italians left this morning by train.

Other detachments, including the Russian, French, and German, immediately follow.

Sir C. MacDonald to the Marquess of Salisbury
(*received June* 11)

My Lord,   *Peking, April* 16, 1900
In my despatch of the 16th ultimo I enclosed a copy of the identical note addressed to the Yamên on the 10th March by myself and my colleagues of the United States, Germany, Italy, and France, reiterating our former demand for the publication in the Official Gazette of a Decree prohibiting certain anti-Christian Societies.

More than three weeks passed without a reply, and on the return of M. Pichon, the French Minister, from a visit to the south, a meeting of the five foreign Representatives was held on the 4th instant, at which it was decided that we should send the Chinese Secretaries of our respective Legations to the Tsung-li Yamên next day with a message to the effect that each of us expected to receive an answer within two days.

This was accordingly done, and on the 7th instant we received the note, of which I have the honour to enclose translation herewith. Although not entirely satisfactory in substance, this note contained an indication that the Chinese Government were prepared to meet our wishes as far as possible.

In acknowledging the receipt of the Yamên's note, which we did in similar terms on the 12th instant, we agreed not to press further for a special Decree in the Gazette, in view of the difficulties described by the Yamên; but at the same time we declared that we held the Chinese Government responsible for any further results which might follow their failure to comply with the measure we had recommended.

I had myself previously suggested informally to the Yamên that a way out of their difficulty might be found by the publication in the "Gazette" of Memorials from the Governor-General of Chihli and Governor of Shantung, respectively, embodying and reporting their action on the Imperial Decree denouncing the Societies which had already been issued at the instance of the Tsung-li Yamên.

For a translation of this satisfactory Decree, as embodied in a Proclamation of the Governor-General of Chihli, I have the honour to refer your Lordship to the Yamên's note of the 1st March enclosed in my despatch of the 5th March. The Governor of Shantung's Proclamation quoting the same Decree had also been sent to myself and my colleagues by the Yamên in a note of the 15th ultimo, of which I enclose translation herewith.

The Yamên have made no reference to my suggestion; but in the "Peking Gazette" of the 14th instant, there was published the Memorial from the Governor-General of Chihli, of which I have the honour to forward a translation to your Lordship. A similar Memorial from the Governor of Shantung may be expected to follow in due course.

In any case the fact that an Imperial Decree denouncing the "Boxers" or "Fist of Righteous Harmony" by name has appeared in the Gazette may be accepted as a practical concession of the demands made by my colleagues and myself, our only object all along having been to secure for such a Decree a publicity equal to that accorded to the disturbing and ambiguous Edict of the 11th January. It is true that the Ta Tao Hui ("Big Knife Society") is not mentioned by name, but all my recent information goes to show that I Ho Ch'üan ("Fist of Righteous Harmony") and Ta Tao Hui are but different titles of the same organization, and I therefore attach no significance to this omission.

I had the honour to report to your Lordship by telegraph to-day the publication of this Decree.

As an example of the constant reluctance of the Tsung-li Yamên to admit being influenced by the requests made by foreign Legations, I may instance a recent case in which representations made by me were apparently passed over in silence, although the result at which I aimed was in reality effected.

At the instance of Her Majesty's Consul at Tientsin I called the attention of the Yamên, on the 5th March, to the fact that the Magistrate of Tsaoch'iang, whose dismissal from his post had been promised me by the Viceroy of Chihli as a punishment for his gross neglect of duty in connection with "Boxer" disturbances in his district, had been allowed by the Provincial Treasurer to take leave under plea of illness.

I pointed out that, in view of the expressed intention of the Throne of China to adopt effective measures for the complete suppression of the Societies in question, it amounted to an exhibition of extreme leniency to permit a Magistrate, guilty of allowing rebellious characters to escape and of neglecting to make arrests, simply to leave his post on the plea of sickness; and I requested that the Viceroy should be directed to carry out his original intention in dealing with this officer.

The Yamên made no reply to my communication; but a Memorial from the Viceroy of Chihli, published in one of the editions of the "Gazette" of the 2nd instant, has come to my notice, in which the Magistrate in question is severely denounced for conniving at the escape of the "Boxer" leader, whom he ought to have caught last January. The Imperial rescript to the Memorial orders him to be deprived of his rank.

I regret to have to conclude by stating that the continued activity of the "Boxer" Society in drilling and enlisting recruits in the neighbourhood of Peking and Tien-tsin indicates that the danger from this source is not yet passed; but, at the same time, I think I am justified in expressing the opinion that the Central Government is at last beginning to give evidence of a genuine desire to suppress this anti-Christian organization.

CLAUDE M. MacDONALD

Enclosure 1
The Tsung-li Yamên to Sir C. MacDonald
(Translation)

Sir,   *Peking, April* 7, 1900

The Yamên have the honour to acknowledge the receipt on the 10th of the moon (10th March) of your Excellency's despatch, requesting the insertion in the "Peking Gazette" of an Imperial Decree with regard to the "Fist of Righteous Harmony" and "Big Knife" Societies.

[Despatch summarized]

The Yamên have the honour to observe that, in the course of the first moon (February), they presented a Memorial to the Throne praying for the prohibition of the "Fist of Righteous Harmony" and the "Big Knife" Society, and had the honour to receive a Decree directing the Viceroy of Chihli and the Governor of Shantung to publish Proclamations. In these Proclamations, as stated by the Yamên in previous despatches, the Imperial Decree is quoted textually in full, while in that published by the Governor of Shantung the "Big Knife" Society is specified by name.

Thus it is evident that the important points covered by your Excellency's request have been already thoroughly dealt with by the Yamên as desired.

With regard to the Imperial Decree previously received, as it has already been directly transmitted to the provinces concerned as a message from the Throne ("t'ing chi": see Yamên's note of the 7th March), it is obviously out of the question that it should be again handed to the Grand Secretariat for publication in the "Peking Gazette". [On this point] the Yamên have already stated the true facts in their previous despatch. The matter is one affected by Standing Regulations, and the Yamên believe that your Excellency will have appreciated their difficulties with regard to it. However, they will not fail, as soon as they have an opportunity, to take into further consideration what can be done to carry out the view expressed in your Excellency's despatch.

(Seal of Yamên)

Enclosure 2

The Tsung-li Yamên to Sir C. MacDonald

(Translation)

Sir,   *Peking, March* 15, 1900

On the 11th instant we received the following communication from the Acting Governor of Shantung:

"On the 22nd February I had the honour to receive the Imperial Edict severely denouncing the Society of the 'Fist of Righteous Harmony,' etc.

"With reference to this, I have to report that in the month of January last, after my arrival at my post, I had already issued a Proclamation vigorously denouncing Boxer Societies, and published it throughout my jurisdiction. In obedience to the Imperial commands now received, I have, as in duty bound, again issued a trenchant Proclamation, and have expressly composed an ode in verses of five characters to be posted from village to village. I have also commanded the local authorities to lead the way in this matter with the gentry, Elders and Headmen of the towns and villages, and on all the market days to expound the ode carefully and truly."

With reference to the above communication, we beg to observe that in the ode composed by the Acting Governor the name of the "Big Knife" Society is definitely mentioned, and that the local authorities are to lead the gentry and Elders in expounding the ode on market days. This is a course of action indicating special zeal and sincerity.

We have the honour to forward herewith, for your Excellency's information, a copy of the draft of the Proclamation and of the ode referred to.

(Seal of Yamên)

Enclosure 3

Proclamation by Yüan, Acting Governor of Shantung
(Translation)
A stringent Proclamation and Admonition issued in obedience to Imperial commands.

On the 23rd February, 1900, a message was reverently received from the Grand Council transmitting the following Imperial Decree, received on the 20th February, 1900.

[Here follows Imperial Decree, as embodied in the Governor-General of Chihli's Proclamation.]

On receipt of the above message it was immediately, in obedience to the Imperial commands, reverently written out and circulated. Again, on the 25th February, I had the honour to receive a communication from the Tsung-li Yamên forwarding a copy of their original Memorial and a copy of the Imperial Decree.

With reference to the above communications I have to observe that in the month of January last I printed a Proclamation strictly prohibiting the Society of the "Fist of Righteous Harmony," and issued it to be posted everywhere throughout my jurisdiction, that every household and every inhabitant might be made aware of its contents, and that evil practices might be eradicated.

Having now had the honour to receive the further commands above set forth, I have instructed all the officers under my jurisdiction to make continual and vigorous investigation and suppress this evil. To this end I have also expressly composed an ode in verses of five characters, and ordered it to be posted from village to village throughout my jurisdiction for the information of all. I have likewise commanded the local authorities, directing the gentry, Elders, and Headmen of the towns and villages on all occasions of public gatherings to engage the services of lecturers, and at the country and town markets and places frequented by traders and people to expound the contents of this ode carefully and accurately, and to exhort and admonish as required.

In addition to this a copy can be issued to every school and college, large or small, and the students directed to chant the ode from time to time. In this way the ode will be published throughout every village community, and even the women and children will know it. The natural disposition of men for good will thus assert itself and all will be clearly made to understand that they cannot believe in or follow after perverse Societies, and that the Imperial Decree cannot be disobeyed.

It is my most earnest hope that those who are already members of the Societies will tremble for the consequences, and those who are not members take warning from the fate of those in front of you; that both may strive to follow righteousness, and that joy and prosperity may be your reward.

Enclosure 4

Extract from the "Peking Gazette" of April 14, 1900
(Translation)

SUPPLEMENTARY MEMORIAL BY YÜ LU
(GOVERNOR-GENERAL OF CHIHLI)

On the 20th day of the first moon of the present year (19th February, 1900), Memorialist had the honour to receive the following Imperial Decree:

[Here follows Decree as embodied in Yü Lu's Proclamation enclosed in Yamên's note of the 1st March.]

Memorialist humbly submits that having learned some time ago that the Society of the "Fist of Righteous Harmony" (or "Boxers") had spread from Shantung into Chihli, in the neighbourhood of Ho-chien-fu, Shên-chou, and Chichou-Chihli districts bordering upon Shantung, that these centres had been established for the practice of boxing and that outrages were being committed on native converts, he immediately gave orders to Mei Tung-li, now Provincial Commander-in-chief of Kuei-chou, then commanding the right wing of the Huai army, and to Chang Lien Fên, expectant Taotai, to lead their forces to the scene, and in conjunction with the local officials acting under their directions, to suppress effectually and disperse (the rioters), and to station troops for the protection of places where there were Christian churches (or missionary establishments).

On repeated occasions the above-mentioned General and his colleague destroyed "Boxer" headquarters by fire and arrested ringleaders of the disturbances, and handed them over to the local officials, by whom they were punished.

As for the ignorant folk, who had been enticed by evil-doers, to enter these societies and learn the "Boxers' " arts, they were ordered to find proper securities that they should in future refrain from such practices. Orders were also given to the local authorities that cases arising between converts and ordinary people should be promptly and impartially settled.

On receipt of the Decree above referred to, Memorialist has at once had the Imperial commands reverently transcribed, and has embodied them in a clearly worded prohibitory Proclamation, which has been issued to every Department and district and posted up everywhere. Orders have also been given to the bodies of troops stationed at various points throughout Memorialist's jurisdiction to act with energy in effecting arrests. If any secret Societies are organized or centres established for the practice of boxing, they are to be immediately and in every case suppressed, and not the slightest remissness is to be exhibited.

The above supplementary Memorial reporting the action taken in obedience to the Imperial Decree, and the issue of a Proclamation strictly prohibiting the "Boxer" Societies is hereby humbly submitted for the inspection of the Throne and the Imperial commands are solicited thereon.

Imperial Rescript

NOTED   It is hereby commanded that the utmost vigilance be shown in the work of suppression in every case, and that not the slightest remissness be permitted.

Sir C. MacDonald to the Marquess of Salisbury
(*received June* 11)

My Lord,   *Peking, April* 18, 1900
In continuation of my despatch of the 16th instant, I have the honour to forward herewith to your Lordship a translation of an Imperial Decree which has since appeared in the "Peking Gazette" deprecating anti-Christian disturbances.

No Societies are mentioned by name; but the reference to those village associations for self defence, which were spoken of with approval in the Decree of the 11th January, seems to indicate that this Decree is intended to correct the mischievous interpretation which had been put upon the former one.

CLAUDE M. MACDONALD

Enclosure

Extract from the "Peking Gazette" of April 17, 1900 (Translation)

IMPERIAL DECREE

The organization of trained bands in village communities throughout the provinces for self-preservation and protection of the inhabitants and their families has its foundation in the fitting principle enjoined by the ancients of "keeping mutual watch and giving mutual help," and, provided that the villagers are peaceful and abide by the law, there is no reason why they should not be allowed to act in this regard at their discretion.

But there is reason to fear that, the good and the evil being indiscriminately associated together in this way, there may be found some who make a pretext (of such organizations) to oppress converts, ignoring the fact that the Throne sets no bounds to its principle of regarding all men with equal benevolence. It is the duty of our subjects humbly to carry this principle into effect, and not to find vent for their private resentments, and so to create disturbances, and involve themselves in crime and punishment.

The High Provincial authorities are hereby commanded to give strict orders to the local officials under them to take every opportunity of making it clearly known to all that every man must attend to his own business, and live continually at peace with his fellow men, that so the reiterated and solemn injunction of the Throne may not be disregarded.

Consul Carles to the Marquess of Salisbury
(*received June* 11)

(Telegraphic)   *Tien-tsin, June* 10, 1900
This morning the second detachment, consisting of British, Germans, Japanese, French, and Russians, numbering about 600 in all, left for Peking. The total force sent was about 1,400 to 1,500 men. There is an interruption in the telegraphic communication with Peking.

Consul Carles to the Marquess of Salisbury
(*received June* 11)

(Telegraphic)   *Tien-tsin, June* 11, 1900
Yesterday evening Admiral Seymour had advanced 30 miles with 1,078 men. He had met with no opposition, and he hopes, unless opposed, to reach Peking this evening. Probably total force is not less than 1,700 men. Last night the train reached Lofa Station.

Admiralty to Foreign Office (received June 11)

Sir,   *June* 11, 1900

With reference to your letter of the 9th instant, I am commanded by my Lords Commissioners of the Admiralty to transmit, for the information of the Secretary of State for Foreign Affairs, copy of a telegram, dated the 11th June, which has this day been sent to the Commander-in-chief on the China station relative to the protection of the Spanish Legation at Peking.

EVAN MACGREGOR

Enclosure

Admiralty to Vice-Admiral Sir E. Seymour

(Telegraphic)   *June* 11, 1900

Afford protection to Spanish Legation at Peking on application from British Minister.

Admiralty to Foreign Office (received June 11)

Sir,   *June* 11, 1900

With reference to Admiralty letter of to-day, I am commanded by my Lords Commissioners of the Admiralty to transmit, for the information of the Secretary of State for Foreign Affairs, a copy of a telegram, dated the 11th June, from Her Majesty's Consul at Tien-tsin, relative to the state of affairs in China.

EVAN MACGREGOR

Enclosure
Consul Carles to Admiralty

(Telegraphic)   *Tien-tsin, June* 11, 1900

Following received from Admiral for transmission:

"Force now increased by 450 Germans, 90 British."

Sir C. MacDonald to the Marquess of Salisbury
(*received June* 12)

(Telegraphic)   *Peking, June* 11, 1900

It is reported that Admiral's party is at Langfang, half-way from Tien-tsin. All communication by telegraph with the latter place is interrupted.

On the 8th June the Boxers attacked student interpreters close to the city walls, who only escaped by using fire-arms.

Some soldiers yesterday assaulted the Secretary of the Belgian Legation at the end of Legation Street.

The summer Legation at the hills which I had officially handed over to the Chinese Government was last night totally destroyed by fire.

I am sending this telegram by the Kiachta route.

Admiralty to Foreign Office (*received June* 12)

Sir,   *June* 12, 1900

I am commanded by my Lords Commissioners of the Admiralty to transmit, for the information of the Secretary of State for Foreign Affairs, a copy of a telegram, dated the 12th June, from the Commander-in-chief, China, relative to the Boxer rising.

EVAN MACGREGOR

Enclosure

Vice-Admiral Sir E. Seymour to Admiralty

(Telegraphic)   *Tien-tsin, June* 12, 1900

Now nearly half-way to Peking; progress much delayed by damage still being done to railway as we advance.

Boxers found in considerable force yesterday afternoon near railway at Langfang, and were engaged. They fled, leaving about thirty-five killed.

No casualties on our side. Our force, increased by 200 Russians and fifty-eight French, who arrived yesterday, is now 2,000 strong.

Sir C. Scott to the Marquess of Salisbury
(received June 12)

(Telegraphic)   *St. Petersburgh, June* 12, 1900

The latest report received from the Russian Minister at Peking, dated the 10th June, confirms the alarming account of the situation there given in Sir C. MacDonald's telegrams of the 8th instant. An audience has not apparently been granted to the foreign Ministers, the Boxers have entered the capital, and the situation is one of danger for the Legations.

In Count Mouravieff's opinion, the real state of things has been concealed from the Empress-Dowager, and, since all the Chinese Councillors having any experience of Europe have been removed, there is none in authority on whose influence it is possible to place any reliance.

Authority has been given to M. de Giers to order up immediately any amount of military force he may consider necessary; but his Excellency understands that, while a very large additional force has been sent by us from Tien-tsin, Russia has only sent up thirty more men.

I replied that, according to the latest telegrams which I had seen from Tien-tsin, all the Commanders were dispatching sufficient forces to restore railway communication with the capital and keep it open, and to secure the safety of the foreign Legations, the primary importance of which his Excellency admitted.

Consul Carles to the Marquess of Salisbury
(received June 12)

(Telegraphic)   *Tien-tsin, June* 12, 1900
Yesterday a further detachment of 300 men passed up. The total force which had left Tien-tsin up to last night is estimated to number 2,300.

Sir C. MacDonald to the Marquess of Salisbury
(received June 13)

(Telegraphic)   *Peking, June* 12, 1900
Pressing. Inform relief party the mutinous Kansu soldiery, who are to-day in possession of the Peking terminus, may offer them some resistance there. The Government of China seems powerless. It is useless to wait till troops arrive from Singapore; if necessary, I hope Admirals will not have the least hesitation in depleting their ships.

Consul Carles to the Marquess of Salisbury
(received June 13)

(Telegraphic)   *Tien-tsin, June* 12, 1900

The Admiral, who had been fighting with the Boxers yesterday, killing about fifty of them, was at Langfang this morning. Our side suffered no loss. The above-mentioned place is half-way on the road to Peking.

Admiralty to Foreign Office (received June 13)

Sir,   *June* 13, 1900

I am commanded by my Lords Commissioners of the Admiralty to transmit, for the information of the Secretary of State for Foreign Affairs, a copy of a telegram, dated the 13th June, from the Commander-in-chief on the China station relative to the Boxer rising.

EVAN MACGREGOR

Enclosure

Vice-Admiral Sir E. Seymour to Admiralty

(Telegraphic)   *Tien-tsin, June* 13, 1900

Progress very slow; railway much broken up, only 3 miles during last twenty-four hours.

No further encounter with Boxers, who are said to be 2 miles in advance in force.

The Russians are landing an additional force of 1,700 troops, and I have requested General to send 650 troops now ready at Hong Kong to Taku in "Terrible."

Trustworthy courier arrived from Peking reports great excitement there at our approach.

General Tung expected to oppose entry within city.

Mr Herbert to the Marquess of Salisbury
(*received June* 13)

(Telegraphic)   *Paris, June* 13, 1900
Although last telegram received from French Minister at Peking was dated yesterday, M. Delcassé has received no news of presence of Boxers in the capital, reported in Sir C. Scott's telegram of 12th June.

Sir C. Scott to the Marquess of Salisbury
(*received June* 13)

(Telegraphic)   *St. Petersburgh, June* 13, 1900
Count Mouravieff, at his reception to-day, appeared to consider that, owing to the agitation of the Reform party, the situation was really more threatening in Southern and Central than in Northern China.

His Excellency counts on the large European force which is now forcing its way to Peking as sufficient to save the situation in the capital.

In his opinion, the Empress-Dowager is at the present moment powerless in the hands of fanatic and ignorant councillors, but she will be both willing to assist and amenable to sounder views when once she has been relieved from their control.

The foreign Representatives on the spot were possessed of the views of their respective

Governments as to the necessity of not further endangering or complicating a position of affairs already very serious, and events were moving so rapidly that the only thing to be done was to trust to their judgment and prudence.

Mr Whitehead to the Marquess of Salisbury
(*received June* 13)

(Telegraphic)   *Tôkiô, June* 13, 1900
Information has reached here that 1,700 Russian soldiers were landed yesterday at Taku, including 270 cavalry and 20 guns. Two more ships had arrived with a further contingent of 1,000 men.

The Minister for Foreign Affairs has inquired as to the intention of Her Majesty's Government, and wished to know whether British troops can be sent. He said that if foreign naval detachments which have been actually landed should be surrounded or otherwise in danger, the Japanese Government would be ready to send at once a considerable force to their relief, if Her Majesty's Government concurred in such a course, but that otherwise his Government do not intend to send soldiers.

Consul Carles to the Marquess of Salisbury
(*received June* 13)

(Telegraphic)   *Tien-tsin, June* 13, 1900
A member of Japanese Legation at Peking, when on his way to station, was killed by General Tung's cavalry, and I believe that Her Majesty's summer Legation has been destroyed by fire. In private letters,

dated Peking, the 11th instant, the situation is described as being extremely grave.

Prince Tuan and three other Manchu Ministers have been made members of the Tsung-li Yamên.

Lack of water, and continued injury to railway, delays to a great extent the advance of Naval Brigade, whose entry into Peking the Chinese expect will be resisted. I fear that the delay in their progress makes this more probable than before.

General Officer Commanding, Hong Kong, to the Secretary of State for War
(communicated by War Office, June 13)

(Telegraphic) *Hong Kong, June* 13, 1900
I am sending 950 British and Indian troops, with Maxim and gun, to the Admiral, who has asked for every man available. Some will leave on the 14th instant, on a fast transport vessel; the rest on the 17th instant on Her Majesty's ship "Terrible." The absence of these troops does not compel me to ask for reinforcements at once.

Admiralty to Foreign Office (received June 14)

Sir, *June* 13, 1900
I am commanded by my Lords Commissioners of the Admiralty to request you will inform the Secretary of State that the following is a summary of the international forces now under the command of Vice-Admiral Sir Edward Seymour on their way to Peking, compiled from telegrams which have been received from him from time to time:

British	736
German	450
American	100
Russian	315
French	158
Austrian	25
Italian	40
Japanese	52
Total	1,876

It will, however, be observed that this does not agree with the total of 2,000 mentioned by the Vice-Admiral in his telegram of the 12th instant, copy of which has already been sent to you.

C. J. THOMAS
Pro Sec.

Sir C. MacDonald to the Marquess of Salisbury
(received June 14)

(Telegraphic)   *Peking, June* 14, 1900
I am informed by Russian Minister that 2,000 men embarked at Port Arthur for Taku on 11th June. More probably the date should be 9th June.

The Japanese Secretary of Legation was killed yesterday by Tartar cavalry close to the city gate.

It may be assumed that the Japanese will also send troops to Taku.

Consul Carles to the Marquess of Salisbury
(received June 14)

(Telegraphic)   *Tien-tsin, June* 14, 1900
I have received a letter from Sir C. MacDonald,
written on the 12th instant in which he informs me
that Ministers of Yamên had called to say that, if the
force did not exceed 1,200 men, Chinese
Government would not oppose their coming to
Peking.

Consul Carles to the Marquess of Salisbury
(received June 14)

(Telegraphic)   *Tien-tsin, June* 14, 1900
A report, which I do not think it right to disregard,
has reached me from Chinese sources that on the
16th June the Empress-Dowager has resolved to
destroy the Legations. Boxers here very menacing,
and I understand that two bridges beyond Yang-tsun
have been rendered impassable. Communications
with Admiral are interrupted.

Acting Consul-General Warren to the Marquess of
Salisbury (received June 14)

(Telegraphic)   *Shanghae, June* 14, 1900
I have received no exact information as to the situation in the north, but news seems to be worse.

I am convinced that, if there is any likelihood of
it resulting in a breach with the Peking Government,
we ought at once to come to an understanding with
the Hankow and Nanking Viceroys. I have every confidence that they will do all they can to keep peace in

their districts if they can rely on Her Majesty's Government for effective support.

There is no doubt that great loss would be caused and probably considerable loss of life would be entailed by any outbreak in the Yang-tsze Valley. It is necessary that prompt action should be taken; the situation is serious.

The Marquess of Salisbury to Mr Whitehead
(Telegraphic)   *Foreign Office, June* 14, 1900
China crisis: your telegram of the 13th June.
You should inform Japanese Minister for Foreign Affairs of the application for troops made by our Admiral, and of the numbers which are being sent from Hong Kong.

Admiralty to Rear-Admiral Bruce
(*communicated by Admiralty, June* 15)
(Telegraphic)   *June* 15, 1900
Adequate means for protecting life and property on Yang-tsze should be provided, using ships from Philippines and Southern Division for this purpose.

Take action and inform Commander-in-chief when you can.

Consul Carles to the Marquess of Salisbury
(*received June* 15)
(Telegraphic)   *Tien-tsin, June* 15, 1900
The native city is practically in the hands of the Boxers and the mob, who have burnt down the

chapels and compelled Chinese officials to get out of their chairs in the streets.

The action of the Viceroy has been very correct.

Communication with the Admiral is cut off.

The situation here is more serious than he is aware of.

A portion of the Russian troops still remains in this place.

Consul Carles to the Marquess of Salisbury
(received June 15)

(Telegraphic)   *Tien-tsin, June* 15, 1900

The Chinese Government are taking measures to concentrate troops along the approaches to Tien-tsin and on Taku.

I am informed that, in consequence of this, the Admirals may be compelled to seize the Taku forts without delay.

Consul Carles to the Marquess of Salisbury
(received June 15)

(Telegraphic)   *Tien-tsin, June* 15, 1900

On the evening of 13th June the Boxers entered Peking and destroyed the old Custom-house quarters and the establishments of several Missions.

It appears that many Chinese were massacred, but that there were no casualties among the Europeans.

The Marquess of Salisbury to Mr Whitehead

(Telegraphic)   *Foreign Office, June* 15, 1900

Murder by Chinese troops of the Chancellor of the Japanese Legation at Peking.

Inquire what steps, if any, the Japanese Government contemplate taking.

The Marquess of Salisbury to Acting Consul-General Warren

(Telegraphic)   *Foreign Office, June* 15, 1900

Protection of British interests on the Yang-tsze.

Your telegram of the 14th June.

We are in communication with the Admiralty as to the dispatch of a man-of-war to Nanking, and the message to the Viceroys there and at Hankow which you suggest, assuring them of British protection in maintaining order.

You are authorized, in the meantime, to inform the Viceroy at Nanking that he will be supported by Her Majesty's ships if measures are taken by him for the maintenance of order.

You should inform Her Majesty's Consul-General at Hankow that he may give to the Viceroy there a similar assurance.

Foreign Office to Admiralty

Sir,   *June* 15, 1900

I am directed by the Marquess of Salisbury to transmit to you, to be laid before the Lords Commissioners of the Admiralty, a copy of a telegram from Her Majesty's Consul at Tien-tsin [dated June 15, 1900] relative to the state of affairs at that place.

Mr Carles reports that the Viceroy has acted very correctly.

In these circumstances his Lordship proposes, should their Lordships see no objection, to instruct Mr Carles to inform the Viceroy that, in the event of his believing himself to be in personal danger, it will be open to him to take refuge on board one of Her Majesty's ships.

FRANCIS BERTIE

Foreign Office to Admiralty

Sir,   *June* 15, 1900

I am directed by the Marquess of Salisbury to transmit to you a copy of a telegram from Shanghae, which has been communicated by the China Association to this Department, relative to the importance of having a sufficient force on the Yang-tsze for the protection of the interests of this country during the present crisis.

Mr Pelham Warren, Acting Consul-General at Shanghae, in his telegram of the 14th instant, of which a copy has been sent to you, also urges the necessity of British interests on the Yang-tsze being efficiently protected, and states that it would, in his opinion, be advisable to send a large man-of-war to Nanking, and to assure the Viceroy that he will receive the support of Her Majesty's Government in maintaining order.

Lord Salisbury concurs in Mr Warren's view as to the desirability of arriving at some understanding on the subject with the Viceroys both at Nanking and Hankow, and he would be glad if arrangements could be made for the dispatch of one of Her Majesty's ships to Nanking with instructions to communicate with the Viceroy in the sense suggested, and for a similar intimation being conveyed to the Viceroy at Hankow.

FRANCIS BERTIE

Enclosure

Telegram from Shanghae Committee to General Committee

With a view to preventing possible disturbance Yang-tsze River, it is very important that there should be adequate force prepared to protect our interests. There are at present above Hankow the "Esk", "Woodlark", "Woodcock", and "Snipe". Nothing below.

Key to the situation—Kiang-yin.

Foreign Office to India Office

Sir,   *June* 15, 1900

In view of the considerable force of British and Indian troops which is being sent from Hong Kong to Taku on the requisition of the Naval Commander-in-chief on the China station, the Marquess of Salisbury desires to submit, for the consideration of the Secretary of State for India, the question of replacing them by the dispatch to Hong Kong of one or two battalions of native troops from India. It is possible that more may be required.

The men who have been landed from the British squadron at Taku cannot be spared for long from the ships; and having regard to the present state of affairs in China, and the impossibility of foreseeing the course which events in the Far East may take, it appears to his Lordship very desirable that the British garrisons should be maintained at their full strength.

A similar letter has been addressed to the War Office.

ST JOHN BRODRICK

Admiralty to Foreign Office (received June 16)

Sir,   June 16, 1900

With reference to your letter of the 15th instant, I am commanded by my Lords Commissioners of the Admiralty to request you to state to the Marquess of Salisbury that they concur in his proposal that in the event of the Viceroy of Tien-tsin being in personal danger on account of his correct attitude, he should be allowed to take refuge on board one of Her Majesty's ships.

Copy of a telegram on the subject which has been this day sent to the Rear-Admiral at Taku is enclosed for information.

H. J. VAN SITTART NEALE

Enclosure

Admiralty to Rear-Admiral Bruce

(Telegraphic)   June 16, 1900

In event of Viceroy, Tien-tsin, being in personal danger owing to his loyalty to British, he is to be afforded an asylum on board one of Her Majesty's ships.

Foreign Office is informing Consul accordingly.

Admiralty to Foreign Office (received June 16)

Sir,   June 16, 1900

In reply to your letter of the 15th instant, I am commanded by my Lords Commissioners of the Admiralty to transmit, for the information of the Secretary of State for Foreign Affairs, copy of a telegram, dated this day, which has been sent to the Senior Naval Officer, Shanghae.

EVAN MACGREGOR

Enclosure

Admiralty to Senior Naval Officer, Shanghae

(Telegraphic)   June 16, 1900

"Hermione" proceed Nanking and communicate with Viceroy, assuring him of support of Her Majesty's Government in preserving order and protecting British interests; in the event of disturbance, consult with Consul, Shanghae, before leaving.

"Linnet" to proceed to Hankow for similar purpose and to give similar assurance to Viceroy there, and to communicate with Consul there.

"Undaunted" leaves Hong Kong to-day for Woosung.

Mr Whitehead to the Marquess of Salisbury
(received June 16)

(Telegraphic)   *Tôkiô, June 16, 1900*

Japanese troops are to leave Ujina on the 21st June, and should arrive about the 24th June at Taku. They will consist of one battalion with two or three guns, making about 1,200 men in all.

The cruiser "Yoshino" left for Taku this morning with Admiral Dewa.

Consul-General Warren to the Marquess of Salisbury
(received June 16)

(Telegraphic)   *Shanghae, June* 16, 1900

The last intelligence we possess is that on the night of the 13th June there were serious disturbances in Peking, when hundreds of converts and servants of foreigners were murdered. It is stated that no Europeans were killed. Many buildings belonging to foreigners were destroyed.

It is not probable that communication with Tientsin, which is now interrupted, will be restored at any early date.

The Marquess of Salisbury to Consul Carles

(Telegraphic)   *Foreign Office, June* 16, 1900

If possible, communicate with Admiral by runner. You should inform him that 950 troops have been ordered to Taku from Hong Kong. You should also ascertain his position, whether he needs reinforcements or supplies, and what his prospects are.

The Marquess of Salisbury to Consul Carles

(Telegraphic)   *Foreign Office, June* 16, 1900

With reference to your telegram of the 15th June, you should inform Viceroy that it is open to him to take refuge on one of Her Majesty's ships in the event of his considering himself in personal danger.

The Marquess of Salisbury to Sir C. MacDonald
Sir,   *Foreign Office, June* 16, 1900
I have received your despatch of the 16th April, reporting further negotiations with the Chinese Government on the subject of anti-Christian Societies in the Provinces of Shantung and Chihli.

I approve your proceedings in the matter.

SALISBURY

The Marquess of Salisbury to Mr Whitehead
Sir,   *Foreign Office, June* 16, 1900
The Japanese Chargé d'Affaires called at this Office on the 11th instant and communicated the substance of a telegram which he had received from Viscount Aoki, instructing him to ascertain the attitude of Her Majesty's Government in the present crisis in China, and to inquire confidentially what action Her Majesty's Government would take should the Chinese Government prove themselves incapable of restoring peace and order and of protecting foreigners in China.

By my direction, Mr Villiers informed Mr Matsui that a force from the various squadrons at Taku was advancing on Peking, and that it was impossible to predict what the position of affairs would be on its arrival; that Her Majesty's Minister and the British Admiral had been left a wide discretion as to the best course to pursue, and that it was the desire of Her Majesty's Government to act with Japan and the other Powers interested in the restoration of order.

SALISBURY

Sir C. Scott to the Marquess of Salisbury
(*received June* 17)

(Telegraphic)   *St. Petersburgh, June* 17, 1900

According to information I have received, either tomorrow or Tuesday the "Official Gazette" will announce the issue of orders for the immediate dispatch of a force from Port Arthur to relieve the situation in Peking; this force will vary from 2,000 to 5,000 strong, according to necessity. A statement of the exact number of troops to be sent will be made on receipt of a telegram which is expected.

An explanation will accompany the announcement to the effect that to co-operate in the general interest for the protection of European lives and property is the sole aim of this expedition, and that it in no way indicates any desire to depart from the Emperor's settled peaceful and unaggressive policy.

Commander Gaunt to Admiralty (*communicated by Admiralty, June* 17)

(Telegraphic)   *Luu-leun-tao, June* 17, 1900

Writing on the evening of the 15th instant, the Rear-Admiral tells me that the Commander-in-chief is cut off 40 miles from Peking by Chinese troops and Boxers. If 2,000 Chinese troops, which were stated to be trying to cut Tien-tsin off from Taku advanced, the Council of Admirals have decided to shell the Taku forts. Her Majesty's ship "Phœnix" is at Chifu, and Her Majesty's ship "Peacock" is here. The telegraphic communication with the north is interrupted.

I send the above because I am in doubt as to whether you have been informed of the present situation.

Count Mouravieff to M. de Staal (communicated by M. de Staal, June 18)

(Translation)

(Telegraphic)   *St. Petersburgh, June* 3 (16), 1900

From the moment of the occurrence of events of an alarming nature in China the Government has exerted every effort to draw the attention of the Chinese Ministers to the dangerous consequences which might result from the excessive national excitement, and to induce the Tsung-li Yamên to adopt more vigorous measures for the re-establishment of order and security in the country.

Unhappily, the friendly counsels of the Russian Representative, as well as those of the other Powers at Peking have failed. The revolt of the Boxers constantly assumes a more menacing aspect. The life and property of foreign subjects are in danger. Finally, the destruction of the railways and the cutting of the telegraph lines has rendered it impossible for the Governments to remain in direct communication with their Legations at Peking.

Consequently, it becomes imperative to take more effective measures to assure the safety of the Imperial Legation and of Russian subjects residing in the country. With this object, His Majesty the Emperor has deigned to order the dispatch of a contingent of 4,000 soldiers, to be placed at the disposal of the Russian Minister at Peking.

The danger of the existing situation is universally recognized.

The British Representative applied to our Legation to ascertain how far the Imperial Government was prepared to co-operate with the efforts now being made to put an end to the existing complications. Certain other colleagues of M. de Giers have on their part solicited the aid and protection of the Russian Legation for their countrymen.

It is agreed that the temporary dispatch of the detachment of Russian troops has for its primary object the security of the Imperial Legation and that of Russian subjects resident in the north of China, and is actuated by no hostile designs with regard to that country, with which we maintain friendly and neighbourly relations.

On the contrary, instructions have been given to the detachment to co-operate with the troops landed by the other Powers, and to assist the Chinese Government at the same time in the work of re-establishing order so necessary, in the primary interests of China herself.

Acting Consul-General Warren to the Marquess of Salisbury (received June 18)

(Telegraphic)   *Shanghae, June* 18, 1900

I have received the following from Her Majesty's Consul at Hankow:

"I have given Lord Salisbury's message verbally to the Viceroy. Should there be disturbances he will apply for assistance. He professed to be confident of the ability of the Nanking Viceroy, with whom he is in communication, and himself to preserve order and to be taking the necessary steps for that purpose."

Lord Pauncefote to the Marquess of Salisbury (received June 18)

(Telegraphic)   *Washington, June* 18, 1900

I learn from the United States' Secretary of State that orders have been sent to an American Regular Regiment now at Manila to proceed to Tien-tsin, and act in concert with the other Powers for the protection of foreign life and property and the suppression of disorder.

They will be accompanied by suitable artillery.

India Office to Foreign Office (received June 19)

Sir,   *June* 18, 1900

I am directed to acknowledge the receipt of your letter of the 15th June, and to state, for the information of the Marquess of Salisbury, that Lord George Hamilton has on a requisition received from the War Office, requested the Government of India to replace the regiments at Hong Kong and Singapore by native regiments from India.

C. STEDMAN, *Major-General*
Military Secretary

Memorandum communicated by Chinese Minister, *June* 19, 1900

The Chinese Minister has been requested by the Viceroy of Huquang to communicate to the Marquess of Salisbury the purport of a telegram which he has just received from his Excellency with reference to a communication which Her Majesty's Consul at Hankow had been instructed to make to the Viceroy on the part of his Lordship.

The communication consisted of an offer of assistance which the Consul said Her Majesty's Government would be prepared to give to the Viceroy in preserving order and tranquillity in the provinces under his jurisdiction, in the event of the "Boxer" movement now agitating the Provinces of Chihli and Shantung extending to those on the Yang-tsze.

The Viceroy tenders his grateful acknowledgments to Lord Salisbury for his friendly offer, and will gladly avail himself of it in case of need. He, however, is persuaded that he and his colleague, the Viceroy of Nanking, with whom he has been in communication on the subject, will be more than able to cope with the "Boxers" or any other elements of disorder who, contrary to his expectations, may attempt to disturb the peace and tranquillity of the Yang-tsze provinces.

Both he and the Viceroy of Nanking have at their disposal very sufficient, well-equipped, and well-disciplined forces, on which they can implicitly depend; and these they will so dispose and employ as to give the fullest measure of protection to all residing within their respective jurisdictions, whether natives or foreigners, and of whatever religion.

Under these circumstances, the Viceroy would deprecate any obtrusive demonstration of British naval force on the Yang-tsze as being calculated rather to make difficulties for the Chinese authorities than to aid them in maintaining tranquillity and good order in the riverine provinces.

Admiralty to Foreign Office (received June 19)

Sir,   *June* 19, 1900

I am commanded by my Lords Commissioners of the Admiralty to transmit, for the information of the Secretary of State for Foreign Affairs, a copy of a telegram, dated the 18th instant, from the Commanding Officer, Her Majesty's ship "Endymion," at Liu-kun-tau, respecting Chinese affairs.

EVAN MACGREGOR

Enclosure

Commanding Officer of "Endymion" to Admiralty

(Telegraphic)   *Liu-kun-tau, June* 18, 1900

Taku forts opened fire at 1 o'clock in the morning of the 17th June on the ships of the allied squadron. After six hours' engagement forts were silenced and occupied by the allied forces. Additional men for storming forts were sent ashore from the ships previous afternoon. British ships up the river engaged were "Algerine," "Fame," and "Whiting." Two latter captured four Chinese torpedo-boat destroyers. Casualties: "Algerine," slight; storming party and others unknown. Chinese second-class cruiser flying Admiral's flag detained outside Taku by the allied Admirals. No information of Commander-in-chief. China's return to Tien-tsin Bay had been received by the Rear-Admiral by 2 P.M., 17th June. Rear-Admiral not desiring to detach Chinese regiment, "Peacock" remains Wei-hai Wei. All British ships at Taku much depleted by men landed. Am leaving at once for Taku.

Mr Whitehead to the Marquess of Salisbury
(received June 19)

(Telegraphic)   *Tôkiô, June* 19, 1900

Besides the troops mentioned in my telegram of 16th June, it is stated by the Japanese Naval Department that, in four or five days, 1,300 additional troops will be sent to Taku.

Admiralty to Foreign Office (received June 20)

Sir,   *June* 20, 1900

I am commanded by my Lords Commissioners of the Admiralty to transmit, for the information of the Secretary of State for Foreign Affairs, a copy of a telegram, dated the 19th instant, from the Commanding Officer, Her Majesty's ship "Hermione," relative to affairs in China.

EVAN MACGREGOR

Enclosure

Commanding Officer of "Hermione" to Admiralty

(Telegraphic)   *Shia-ku-an, June* 19, 1900

I have had interview with Viceroy, and saw telegram received from Viceroy, Hankow, in which latter suggested to him that it is undesirable for any ship to be in Yang-tsze Kiang at present time. Viceroy, Nanking, considered two ships should be sufficient. Viceroy claims they are quite able to preserve order should any disturbance take place, which, they assert, is extremely unlikely.

In my opinion, present strength in Yang-tsze Kiang should not be reduced, and I have made arrangements to send ships to each Treaty port. Purpose leaving 20th June for Wuhu to await arrival of "Snipe" there, then returning to Nanking.

Consul concurs.

Admiralty to Foreign Office (received June 20)

Sir,   June 20, 1900

I am commanded by my Lords Commissioners of the Admiralty to transmit, for the information of the Secretary of State for Foreign Affairs, extract of a telegram, dated 17th–18th June, from Rear-Admiral Bruce.

EVAN MACGREGOR

Enclosure

Rear-Admiral Bruce to Admiralty

(Telegraphic)   *Taku (via Chefoo), June 20, 1900*

June 17. Taku fort captured by allied forces this morning. Bombardment commenced 12.50 A.M., ended about 6.30 A.M. Details later on. Chinese Admiral present with allied fleet; flag flying in cruiser. At Council meeting this morning he agreed to anchor with fleet, putting out fires.

June 18. Situation getting worse. All north China under arms. No news from Commander-in-chief and advanced guard. Tien-tsin now cut off. Heavy fire heard there last night.

My communications with allied authorities most harmonious.

Admiralty to Rear-Admiral Bruce (communicated by Admiralty, June 20)

(Telegraphic)   *June* 20, 1900

Eight hundred seamen and marines leave by freight as soon as possible for Hong Kong to wait orders, and ships on station will be reinforced.

Sir C. Scott to the Marquess of Salisbury
(received June 20)

(Telegraphic)   *St Petersburgh, June* 20, 1900

Count Mouravieff explained to me to-day that the 4,000 troops mentioned in the telegram to the Russian Embassy consist of 2,000 who are understood to be already at Taku or the mouth of the river, and of the 2,000 at Tien-tsin who, last week, while the other foreign troops defended the foreign Settlements, attacked and dispersed with loss the Boxers threatening that town.

For the last four days no direct news from Taku or Tien-tsin, and for seven days no knowledge of the situation at Peking or confirmation of the reported return of Admiral Seymour's expedition, have been received by the Russian Foreign Office, but Count Mouravieff takes a sanguine view of the situation, and appears to expect that not only will communication for news from Tien-tsin and probably Peking be opened up at once by the capture of the Taku forts, but that it will also exercise a salutary impression on the Empress-Dowager, who has been hesitating between her fear of the Boxers and her fear of the intervention of the foreign Powers.

His Excellency still regards the state of things in Central and Southern China as more threatening, and believes that in a fortnight the crisis will be over.

Consul Carles to the Marquess of Salisbury
(received June 20)

(Telegraphic)   *Chefoo, June 20, 1900*

Much damage was done last night to the line north of Tien-tsin by Boxers, and a great number of Chinese houses, together with the Roman Catholic Cathedral and Mission chapel, were burnt. There was no visible effort made to restrain them by the Chinese troops. The Boxers attacked the Settlement, and about 100 were killed by the foreign guard.

Acting Consul-General Fraser to the Marquess of Salisbury
(received June 20)

(Telegraphic)   *Hankow, June 20, 1900*

I am assured by the Viceroy that every possible measure to maintain order is being taken by him and the Viceroy of Nanking, and they have no doubt of their power. In view of the probability of popular alarm and suspicion being caused thereby he deprecates any naval demonstration, though, of course, understanding that this protest does not include the ordinary movements of Her Majesty's ships.

Foreign Office to Admiralty

Sir,   *June 20, 1900*

I am directed by the Marquess of Salisbury to transmit to you, to be laid before the Lords

Commissioners of the Admiralty, a copy of a Memorandum [dated June 19, 1900] given to his Lordship by the Chinese Minister relative to the offer of assistance made by Her Majesty's Government to the Viceroys of Hankow and Nanking in preserving order.

Their Excellencies, while grateful for the offer, consider the forces at their disposal sufficient to cope with any disturbances which may arise, and deprecate any obtrusive demonstration on the part of the British naval force.

I am to suggest that instructions be issued to the Officer Commanding Her Majesty's ships on the Yang-tsze River to avoid any demonstrations, but to inform the Viceroys that Her Majesty's ships will be ready to co-operate with them whenever co-operation becomes necessary for the protection of the lives and property of Europeans, or to support the measures taken by the Viceroys for the maintenance of order.

FRANCIS BERTIE

Admiralty to Foreign Office (received June 21)

Sir   *June 21, 1900*

I am commanded by my Lords Commissioners of the Admiralty to transmit, for the information of the Secretary of State for Foreign Affairs, a decypher of a telegram, dated the 21st instant, from the Rear-Admiral on the China Station relative to affairs in China.

EVAN MACGREGOR

Enclosure

Rear-Adminal, Taku, to Admiralty

(Telegraphic)   *Chefoo, June* 21, 1900

Latest information from Tien-tsin by runner, 20th June.

Reinforcements most urgently required. Casualties have been heavy. Supplies of ammunition insufficient. Machine-guns or field-guns required. Beware ambuscades [ambush] near Tien-tsin. Russians at railway station hard pressed. Chinese maintain incessant fire with large guns on European Concession, nearly all of which burnt.

There are not reinforcements to send.

Admiralty to Foreign Office (received June 21)

Sir,   *June* 21, 1900

I am commanded by my Lords Commissioners of the Admiralty to transmit, for the information of the Secretary of State for Foreign Affairs, a copy of a telegram, dated this day, from the Rear-Admiral on the China Station, relative to affairs in China.

EVAN MACGREGOR

Enclosure

Rear-Admiral Bruce to Admiralty

(Telegraphic)   *Taku, viâ Chefoo, June* 21, 1900

No communication from Commander-in-chief for seven days or with Tien-tsin for five days. Allies hold Taku forts and Tongku securely, and they will advance for relief of Tien-tsin when in sufficient strength.

Troops expected from Hong Kong tomorrow, and 300 from Wei-hai Wei day after to-morrow.

Believe that fighting is constantly going on around Tien-tsin. Our garrison there should be about 3,000.

Following Proclamation was agreed to this morning, to be at once [issued]:

"The Admirals and Senior Naval Officers of the allied Powers in China desire, to make known to all Viceroys and authorities of the coasts and rivers, cities, and provinces of China that they intend to use armed force only against Boxers and peoples who oppose them on their march to Peking for the rescue of their fellow-countrymen."

The Marquess of Salisbury to Sir Chihchen Lofêngluh
Sir,   *Foreign Office, June* 21, 1900
I have received a letter from the Upper Yang-tsze Syndicate (Limited), stating that they are anxious with regard to the safety of their staff now employed in the Province of Szechuen. Their staff consists of Mr Archibald Little, Mr Herbert Way, and Mr James W. Nicolson, and the last news received was a telegram from Mr Way, dated Chengtu, the 17th instant.

I have received a similar communication from Mr W. Pritchard-Morgan relative to Dr Jack and his assistants, Messrs Robert Jack, J. F. Morris, and T. H. Bush, who are employed by him in the same province. The latest news received from Dr Jack was dated Chengtu, the 16th instant.

I have the honour to request that, if you are able to communicate with the Viceroy at Hankow, you will be so good as to inform him by telegraph that the above-mentioned gentlemen are within the limits of his authority, and to request his Excellency to take measures for their protection.

SALISBURY

Foreign Office to Admiralty

Sir,   *June* 21, 1900

With reference to the telegram from the Officer Commanding. Her Majesty's ship "Hermione," of which a copy was enclosed in your letter of the 20th instant, reporting the result of an interview with the Viceroy of Nanking relative to the preservation of order on the Yang-tsze, I am directed by the Marquess of Salisbury to request you to inform the Lords Commissioners of the Admiralty that his Lordship concurs in the opinion expressed by Captain Cumming, that the present strength of the British naval force on the Yang-tsze should not be reduced. Lord Salisbury would further suggest that the arrangements made by Captain Cumming for sending a ship to each Treaty port should be approved.

FRANCIS BERTIE

Consul Carles to the Marquess of Salisbury
(received June 22)

(Telegraphic)   *Tien-tsin viâ Chefoo*
June 21, 1900

June 18.   No news yet received from the front. We have been attacked at various points, but have repelled the enemy.

The Chinese commenced shelling the Settlement yesterday afternoon at 3 o'clock, and a few buildings were slightly damaged. A force composed of Austrians, British, Germans, and Italians, and numbering 175, attacked the Military College, destroyed the guns, killed nearly all the occupants, and finally burnt the College, in which there was a considerable and valuable store of ammunition.

The behaviour of the Russians, who were throughout the day engaged in various quarters, was splendid, and their large force and heavy field-guns, of which they had four, saved the situation. During the day all were engaged on their respective sections. The following is list of casualties: Russians, 7 killed, 5 wounded; British, 1 killed, 5 wounded; Italians, 2 wounded; Germans, 1 killed.

Last night an attempt was made by the Chinese to seize a bridge of boats, but they were repulsed with loss, which included, it is said, one of their Generals.

Our communications have been cut.

Admiralty to Senior Naval Officer, Woosung
(communicated by Admiralty, June 22)

(Telegraphic)   June 22, 1900

With reference to Admiralty telegram of the 16th June to Senior Naval Officer, Shanghae, and with reference to telegram from "Hermione" of the 19th June to Admiralty, instruct Commanding Officers of Her Majesty's ships at Nanking and Hankow to avoid any obtrusive demonstration of naval force on the river, but to inform the Viceroys that Her Majesty's ships will be ready to co-operate with them whenever co-operation becomes necessary for the protection of European life and property, or in support of the measures taken by them for the maintenance of order.

Mr Whitehead to the Marquess of Salisbury
(received June 22)

(Telegraphic)   *Tôkiô, June* 22, 1900

I learn that eleven large steamers averaging 3,000 tons gross, and four small steamers of 400 tons gross, have been chartered by the Japanese Government; of these, six of the large ones are to be used as colliers and store-ships for the navy, the remainder to serve as transports of the troops.

The "Akitsusima" has been dispatched to Chefoo to protect the telegraph.

According to the Foreign Minister, there is no present intention on the part of Japan of sending any more troops than the 3,000 now *en route* to Taku.

The Marquess of Salisbury to Mr Whitehead
(Telegraphic)   *Foreign Office, June* 22, 1900
You should inform Japanese Minister for Foreign
Affairs of the critical condition of the foreign
Legations at Peking, and also, I fear, of the interna-
tional force sent to relieve them under Admiral
Seymour. State that Her Majesty's Government have
sent orders to the Government of India for the dis-
patch of a considerable number of troops to China,
and ascertain whether it is not the intention of the
Japanese Government to send a further force to their
succour.

The urgency of immediate action and the
favourable geographical situation of Japan makes her
intentions a matter of very grave importance in this
difficulty.

The Marquess of Salisbury to Lord Pauncefote
(Telegraphic)   *Foreign Office, June* 22, 1900
China. Strong appeals are being made to Her
Majesty's Government for reinforcements, and the
crisis at Tien-tsin and Peking appears to be urgent.
Orders have been sent to India for the dispatch of a
considerable body of troops, but some time must
elapse before they can arrive.

You should suggest to Mr Hay that any troops
which it would be possible to send from Manila
would be of very great value, as it is probable that the
United States' Legation is in great danger as well as
those of other Powers.

The Marquess of Salisbury to Acting
Consul-General Warren

(Telegraphic)   *Foreign Office, June* 22, 1900

You should inform Viceroy, with reference to your telegram of to-day's date, that he may count on the fullest support of Her Majesty's ships in any efforts he may make to restore order.

The Marquess of Salisbury to Consul Scott

(Telegraphic)   *Foreign Office, June* 22, 1900

Li Hung-chang's departure from Canton.

The Chinese Minister, at an interview to-day, communicated to me a message which he had received from Li Hung-chang to the effect that he had received a summons to proceed to Peking in order to bring about a solution of the crisis in North China. He wished to know whether, notwithstanding the fact that the Taku forts had fired on the international forces without orders from the Government at Peking, the Powers consider themselves at war with the Chinese Government. His visit to Peking would be without utility if it were considered that a state of war existed. In the contrary event, he felt sure of being able to restore order and to suppress the Boxers.

In reply, I informed the Chinese Minister that there is no reason that it should be considered that a state of war exists if the Taku forts had fired without orders from the Government at Peking, and if the attacks on the international troops are without authority; and I strongly advised that if he could be of use in suppressing disorder, and if he could do so with safety to himself, Li Hung-chang should go to Peking, but that he must be judge as to the risk to be run in doing so.

The Marquess of Salisbury to Sir C. MacDonald
Foreign Office, June 22, 1900

The Chinese Minister called on me this morning, and stated that the Viceroy of Nanking entirely adopted the Memorandum which he handed to me on the 19th instant. He was greatly obliged for our offer of assistance which he would make use of if required, but he was anxious on account of his people to avoid anything like a demonstration.

The Minister went on to say that Li Hung-chang had been ordered to go to Peking, and rather wanted our advice. I strongly advised that he should go there if he could be of any use in suppressing disorder so long as he could do so with safety, but that we should be sorry if his life should be in danger.

I said that he must be the best judge of the risk, as he knew his own countrymen better than I did.

Sir Chihchen replied that Li knew his own countrymen, and was quite convinced of his power of repressing disorder amongst them, and had not the least fear that the Boxers would not submit to him. But before he acted in that sense, he wanted to know, and the Empress also wanted to know, what were the intentions of the Powers and especially of Her Majesty's Government who could influence the Powers with reference to the political conditions after the suppression of the outbreak. What were the changes or revolutions, if any, which the Powers intended to introduce?

I replied by disclaiming energetically any responsibility for the acts of other Powers, but said that Her Majesty's Government had no intention whatever at present of taking any steps to affect the existing political position at Peking. Their one object was to restore order and secure life and property. I was obliged to say that their action could not but be affected by the action of the Chinese Government and in some degree of the other Powers, so that he must take my assurances as not necessarily applying beyond the present time. The sooner the Empress had quelled the disorder which had broken out at Peking, the safer she would be from any such changes as those she apprehended.

The Minister told me that the attack by the Taku forts had been made without any order from above.

I replied that if that were so, and that the attacks on the international troops were without authority, there was no reason for considering that a state of war existed, but I warned him that the destruction of property which had taken place would have to be met by an indemnity on the part of the Chinese Government.

SALISBURY

The Marquess of Salisbury to Mr Herbert

Sir,   *Foreign Office, June* 22, 1900

The French Ambassador came to this Department in the forenoon to-day to inform me of a message received by M. Delcassé from the Viceroy Li, and to inquire what my opinion on it might be.

M. Cambon stated to Mr Bertie that M. Delcassé had spoken to the Chinese Minister at Paris on the grave state of affairs in Yünan, and the perilous position of French officials and private individuals in that province. This had probably caused the Chinese Minister to communicate by telegraph with Li Hung-chang, the result being that the Viceroy had sent a message to M. Delcassé to the following effect:

The Government at Peking had summoned the Viceroy to Peking with the view of bringing about a solution of the crisis in the north of China. He would be ready to go to Peking and take measures for the suppression of the Boxers, and felt confident of his ability to do so, provided that the Powers would not consider themselves in a state of war with the Chinese Government. Li Hung-chang stated that the Taku forts had fired on the international forces without orders from the Government at Peking, but that if notwithstanding this act having been unauthorized the Powers considered themselves at war with China his mission to Peking would be without utility, and he should not go.

Soon after M. Cambon had left the Foreign Office, and just before the meeting of the Cabinet, the Chinese Minister brought to me a message from Li Hung-chang, generally to the same effect as the one sent by his Excellency to M. Delcassé, and I have informed the French Ambassador that the answer which I made was that if the forts at Taku fired without orders from the Government at Peking, and the attacks on the international troops are without authority, there is no reason that it should be considered that a state of war exists; and that if Li Hung-chang thinks that his life will be safe at Peking, and that he can suppress the Boxers and restore order, his mission will be viewed favourably by Her Majesty's Government.

The details of my conversation with Lofêngluh are given in my despatch of today to Sir C. MacDonald, of which I have sent to you a copy.

SALISBURY

Foreign Office to M. Cambon
June 22, 1900

Since I saw your Excellency this morning Lord Salisbury has received from Li Hung-chang a message generally to the same effect as the one sent to M. Delcassé.

Lord Salisbury has replied that if the forts at Taku fired without orders from the Government at Peking, and the attacks on the international troops are without authority, there is no reason that it should be considered that a state of war exists, and that if Li Hung-chang thinks that his life is safe at Peking and that he can suppress the Boxers and restore order his mission will be viewed favourably by Her Majesty's Government.

FRANCIS BERTIE

Sir Chihchen Lofêngluh to the Marquess of Salisbury
(received June 23)

Chinese Legation, June 22, 1900

I have the honour to acknowledge the receipt of your Lordship's letter of yesterday's date, expressing the anxiety felt by the Upper Yang-tsze Syndicate (Limited) and Mr Pritchard-Morgan with regard to the safety of their employees in the Province of Szechuen, and, in reply, I beg leave to inform you that, conformably to your Lordship's request, I have telegraphed to the Viceroy of that province requesting that proper measures may be taken for their protection.

LOFÊNGLUH

Lord Pauncefote to the Marquess of Salisbury
(received June 23)

(Telegraphic)   *Washington, June 23, 1900*

The Secretary of State, to whom I communicated the substance of your telegram of the 22nd instant, informs me that in addition to a full regiment, 300 marines have been ordered from Manila to Tien-tsin, and that telegraphic inquiries are being made as to what further force can be spared. His Excellency states that the Chinese Minister here reports assurances from the Viceroys of their ability to maintain order in their provinces.

The Circular of the French Government to the Powers respecting Li Hung-chang's message has been delivered by the French Ambassador to Mr Hay, who has replied that the United States' Government are favourable to the offer being accepted, and that, all the facts not being known, they do not think that a state of war necessarily exists.

Lord Pauncefote to the Marquess of Salisbury
(received June 23)

(Telegraphic)   *Washington, June* 23, 1900
I am informed by the Chinese Minister that, in reply to his inquiry as to the safety of the United States' Minister, he has received a telegram from the Viceroy of Nanking, dated 22nd June, in the following words:

"All the Ministers are well," but how the news reached the Viceroy he could not say.

Mr Whitehead to the Marquess of Salisbury
(received June 23)

(Telegraphic)   *Tôkiô, June* 23, 1900
At 9 this morning I attended a meeting, convened by the Japanese Minister for Foreign Affairs, of the Representatives of Powers who have naval forces at Taku.

Two telegrams from the Japanese Admiral at Taku describing the extreme gravity of the situation, and urgently demanding the immediate dispatch of troops, were read to us by his Excellency.

The Minister, while refusing to make any sugges-tion himself, said that in view of the imminent danger of the situation and the critical position of interna-tional forces, his Government, desirous of conforming their resolves to those of the Powers interested, were anxious to know what measures our Government proposed to take immediately to meet the actual necessities of the case.

Mr Whitehead to the Marquess of Salisbury
(*received June* 23)

(Telegraphic)   *Tôkiô, June* 23, 1900

I at once personally communicated to the Minister for Foreign Affairs the substance of your telegram of the 22nd instant, which I received after the meeting reported in my immediately preceding telegram. Though doubtful as to what decision would be taken, his Excellency promised to submit it to the Cabinet without delay.

The second time I visited the Foreign Office the Minister said that, of course, Japan has troops at her disposal, but that it was impossible to foresee the consequences of sending them.

Admiralty to Foreign Office (*received June* 24)

Sir,   *June* 24, 1900

I am commanded by my Lords Commissioners of the Admiralty to transmit, for the information of the Secretary of State for Foreign Affairs, a decypher of a telegram, dated the 23rd instant, from the Rear-Admiral, China, at Taku, received viâ Chefoo, relative to affairs in China.

EVAN MACGREGOR

Enclosure

Rear-Admiral Bruce to Admiralty

(Telegraphic)   *Chefoo, June* 23, 1900

Received your telegrams.

The allied Admirals are working in perfect accord with Russian Vice-Admiral as Senior Officer, and as the Council of Admirals has supreme control over all the operations, in order to avoid opportunities of friction, the Officer Commanding land forces should belong to same nation, as Senior Admiral, President of Council, as is case now.

A Russian Major-General, with the Russians, and German second in command, and Captain Warrender, are in charge of the operations from Taku forts for relief of Tien-tsin under general control of Russian Major-General. All Admirals in command are together off Taku bar.

Have just received news that Americans and Russians attempted yesterday to relieve Tien-tsin, and were repulsed by Chinese with some loss. Expect Hong Kong regiments to-morrow, and know of no more reinforcements coming.

Russians have landed altogether about 4,000. Russian Admiral told me yesterday he expected no more troops, Germany has landed about 1,300, and expects no more. Other forces landed besides ours small numerically.

Consul Scott to the Marquess of Salisbury
(received June 24)

(Telegraphic)   *Canton, June* 24, 1900

With reference to your telegram of the 22nd instant:

I had yesterday an interview with Li Hung-chang. That morning he had sent a message to Peking asking for definite instructions as to going or remaining, and saying that, unless the Central Government were prepared beforehand to follow his advice, his Mission to the north would be absolutely futile. According to what his Excellency told me he will remain if the matter is left to his own decision; but that, if he is unconditionally ordered to go, he must do so at any risk.

His Excellency does not expect a reply within a week, as telegraphic communication with Peking and Tien-tsin is closed. I was requested by him to convey to your Lordship his thanks for your thoughtful consideration of his position and for your advice.

Consul Scott to the Marquess of Salisbury
(received June 24)

(Telegraphic)   *Canton, June* 24, 1900

On being informed by the French Consul that he had received official intelligence of the bombardment of the Concessions at Tien-tsin by Government troops, I considered it advisable, in view of the probable effect of the news here, to apply for a gun-boat as a precautionary measure, and to allay excitement and anxiety among the foreign community.

Otherwise the state of things here is fairly quiet.

Sir C. Scott to the Marquess of Salisbury
(received June 24)

(Telegraphic)   *St Petersburgh, June* 24, 1900

Under instructions from his Government yesterday, the French Minister was to inform the Russian Government that his Government had learnt from Canton that Li Hung-chang had been summoned to Peking by the Dowager-Empress, but before proceeding there, he had desired to be informed whether the action at Taku was regarded by the foreign Powers as constituting a state of war with the Chinese Government. The French Government desired to ascertain the view of the Russian Government on the subject.

The opinion of Count Lamsdorff was that, as it was not to be assumed that the Chinese troops were acting on instructions from the Chinese Government, but by compulsion of the Boxers, the Powers were not in a state of war with China.

I met M. de Witte yesterday, and he took the same view as that expressed on Wednesday by Count Mouravieff with regard to the situation in the north of China. The summons to Li Hung-chang he regarded as a favourable sign of the Empress's desire to arrange matters with the Powers.

He said that he expected that before any reinforcements from Europe could arrive the whole trouble would be over.

Rear-Admiral Bruce, at Taku, to Admiralty
(*communicated by Admiralty, June* 25)

(Telegraphic)   *Port Arthur, June* 17, 1900
(Delayed on Chinese lines)

Council of Admirals this morning decided to attack Taku forts 2 o'clock in the morning 17th June, if not previously surrendered, for purpose of trying to relieve Commander-in-chief and allied forces marching on Peking, and situation of affairs at Tien-tsin.

Presented ultimatum to Chinese Governor at Tien-tsin and Commandant of forts this afternoon.

Chinese telegraph lines interrupted. Situation of affairs over all China very critical. Towns on the Yang-tsze-Kiang anxious for protection. Commander-in-chief is still cut off from all communication.

Report arrived to-day that the Legations at Peking have been attacked. Tuan, new Head of Foreign Affairs in China, in my belief is head of the Boxers. [Am] saving such missionaries as I hear reach coast.

Rear-Admiral Bruce to Admiralty
(*communicated by Admiralty, June* 25)

(Telegraphic)   *Chefoo, June* 24, 1900

Total force which left Tien-tsin with Commander-in-chief for Peking about 2,000, composed of detachments of the allied ships.

German and American Flag Captains were with Commander-in-chief.

Captain Bayly, "Aurora," has been the commander, heart and soul, of the defence of Tien-tsin, assisted by Captain Burke, "Orlando."

No action could be possibly taken to relieve the Commander-in-chief, because it was only known he was cut off by Tien-tsin being invested. Tien-tsin has been fighting for its life ever since. It was on receipt of information that Chinese army had ordered trains for attacking Tien-tsin, ravaged Tongku, and were reinforcing Taku, as well as mining the mouth of the Peiho, that it was promptly determined to seize Taku just in time, since when every effort has been made to relieve Tien-tsin.

Have commandeered small coasting steamer for taking troops sick and wounded across the bar and to Wei-hai Wei, where I intend making temporary base hospital and asylum for refuge until South China has settled down.

The Marquess of Salisbury to Sir C. Scott
(Telegraphic)   *Foreign Office, June* 25, 1900
I request that you will inquire of the Russian Minister for Foreign Affairs whether his Government will give their approval to dispatch of a Japanese force of from 20,000 to 30,000 men, if Japanese Government are willing to undertake it, for the restoration of order at Tien-tsin and Peking.

The Marquess of Salisbury to Sir C. Scott

(Telegraphic)   *Foreign Office, June* 25, 1900

In your conversation with the Minister for Foreign Affairs on the subject mentioned in my telegram of to-day, you may draw his Excellency's attention to the following considerations: Her Majesty's Government assume that the Russian Government will further reinforce their troops speedily, and are themselves sending some 10,000 troops from India; but it is clear that these reinforcements will not arrive in time to rescue the two forces at present surrounded or the Legations at Peking.

The Marquess of Salisbury to Mr Whitehead

Sir,   *Foreign Office, June* 25, 1900

The Japanese Chargé d'Affaires requested to see me to-day. He asked me what arrangements the Powers were making with respect to the China crisis. I informed him of the troops that were being sent by the various Powers, and that the officers on the spot were left to arrange with each other the measures that were most suitable for relieving the nationals of the various Powers who were in danger. I pointed out to him that considerable time must elapse before the relief from India or Europe could arrive, and that Japan was situated in a manner more favourable for immediate action. I asked him how long it would take to send a considerable force from Japan. He said that would depend upon the locality in Japan from which the force was sent, but he thought that if all preparations were complete, four days would be required for the passage. He did not, however, intimate that there was any chance of an immediate completion of the preparations. He said that he had received no instructions from his Government, but that, in his own opinion, it was not likely they would send a very large force.

He thought some assurance would be required that there was no objection on the part of other Governments which have interests in the East.

I have telegraphed to St. Petersburgh to ascertain whether the Russians would approve of an expedition of 25,000 or 30,000 troops, and have urged upon the German Government that they should support us in this appeal.

SALISBURY

The Marquess of Salisbury to Viscount Gough
(Telegraphic)   *Foreign Office, June* 26, 1900
The crisis in China.
Please inform Minister for Foreign Affairs that I have telegraphed to Her Majesty's Ambassador at St. Petersburgh to inquire whether the Russian Government would approve of a force of from 20,000 to 30,000 men being sent by Japan to Taku.

I gather from the Japanese Chargé d'Affaires, with whom I had an interview late last night, that his Government, unless they receive some assurance that it will not lead to complications with other Powers interested, will not give effective assistance.

I hope the German Emperor will concur in our wish to procure such an assurance from Russia, and that His Majesty will be willing to lend us his assistance in obtaining it.

Acting Consul-General Warren to the Marquess of Salisbury
(received June 26)

(Telegraphic)   *Shanghae, June* 26, 1900

A telegram has been received from the Governor of Shantung, Yuan-shih-Kai, to the effect that he has frequently sent out scouts to get news, but that, as a rule, the Boxers have killed them all. According to his latest information the foreign Ministers in Peking were unharmed up to the 20th instant.

Mr Whitehead to the Marquess of Salisbury
(received June 26)

(Telegraphic)   *Tôkiô, June* 26, 1900

Japanese reinforcements.

Your telegram of the 22nd instant.

I received official information this morning from the Minister for Foreign Affairs that it has been decided by the Japanese Government to mobilize and hold ready one division, which, including the force already sent, will make a total of about 13,000 men. If emergency arises, he states that transports will be available at any moment.

Sir Chihchen Lofêngluh to the Marquess of Salisbury
(received June 26)

Chinese Legation, June 26, 1900

Referring to my letter of the 22nd instant, I have the honour to inform your Lordship that, in reply to the telegram I sent requesting that special precautions should be taken in the Province of Szechuen for the protection of the foreigners there employed by Mr Pritchard-Morgan and the Upper Yang-tsze Syndicate, I have received the following telegram from his Excellency the Viceroy of Huquang:

"Your telegram has been received, and the Viceroy of Szechuen has been requested to give the desired protection.

"In the Upper and Lower Yang-tsze, the Viceroy of Nanking and myself will, under any circumstances, afford adequate protection to foreign merchants, missionaries, and native Christians residing in our respective Governments. Please assure Lord Salisbury that no apprehension need be entertained as to this."

LOFÊNGLUH

Sir Chihchen Lofêngluh to the Marquess of Salisbury
(received June 26)
Chinese Legation, June 26, 1900

The Chinese Minister presents his compliments to the Marquess of Salisbury, and, at the request of the Viceroy of Huquang, has the honour to communicate to his Lordship the following translation of a telegram he has received from his Excellency, dated 6 A.M., the 23rd June:

The rebels in the northern provinces, called by the name of "Boxers," have, in defiance of the Imperial Decree, overrun and devastated a large tract of country in the vicinity of Peking, taking the lives of many persons, natives as well as foreigners of various nationalities, including a member of the Japanese Legation at Peking.

The present lamentable state of affairs, which the Imperial Government deplore as a national calamity, is doubtless attributable to the culpable negligence of the provincial authorities, who surely could never have foreseen the large proportions which the Boxer movement was fated to take; otherwise they would have suppressed it in the commencement.

I am very apprehensive lest the continued occupation of the Taku forts should lead to a breach of harmonious relations between China and the Treaty Powers. The Empress-Dowager and the Emperor have summoned Li Hung-chang to Peking by telegraph, in order to concert measures with the Government to the end that an understanding may be come to with the Treaty Powers; but a fortnight must necessarily elapse before he can arrive, and meanwhile the Treaty Powers are dispatching additional troops to China, which may have the effect of aggravating the gravity of the situation, and of, perhaps, precipitating matters beyond recall; thus creating new opportunities for other disaffected factions to join the Boxers, or even to act independently of them in their fell work of murder, rapine, and plunder.

The intentions of the Imperial Government are entirely pacific and in favour of friendly relations with the Treaty Powers. This is shown by the absence of any instructions to the provincial authorities to take measures with a view to defence.

You should endeavour to induce the Governments to whom you are accredited to instruct their respective naval Commanders in the neighbourhood of Tien-tsin to remain on the defensive until such time as Li Hung-chang shall have arrived in Peking and memorialized the Throne, with respect to the satisfaction to be given to the Powers. In this way, freed from the dread of drifting into war with them, we shall be at liberty to devote all our energies to the suppression of the rebellion.

The Viceroys of the provinces bordering on the Yang-tsze having taken precautions against the possibility of any troubles occurring within their respective jurisdictions, no apprehension need be entertained as to their ability and readiness to afford the fullest measure of protection to foreigners residing at the riverine ports. It might, however, be otherwise, should hostilities be continued at Tien-tsin.

The situation, then, being so critical, I would impress on you the necessity of your exerting yourself to the utmost in order to induce Great Britain to be forbearing, and not to press matters unduly in the north. The provincial authorities of the central provinces all agree with me as to the extreme desirability of these recommendations being attended to, and join me in requesting you to bring to the notice of the Foreign Secretary all the considerations I have given expression to in this telegram.

Sir Chihchen Lofêngluh to the Marquess of Salisbury
(received June 26)

Chinese Legation, June 26, 1900

With reference to the telegram from the Viceroy of Huquang, dated Woochang, the 23rd June, which I have had the honour of communicating to your Lordship, I beg leave to state that I have received another telegram from his Excellency, instructing me to inform you that the under-mentioned Viceroys and Governors of provinces, being in complete accord with him as to the views expressed by him in the said telegram, have expressed a desire to be considered as co-Signatories with him of that communication:

Li Hung-chang, Viceroy of the Two Kwangs

Lieu Kwun Yih, Viceroy of the Two Kiangs

Wang Chi Chün, Governor of Anhwei

Yüen Shi Kai, Governor of Shantung

Yü Lin San, Governor of Hunan

In requesting your Lordship to take note of this, I venture to express the hope that the adherence of these important functionaries to the telegram of the Viceroy of Huquang may be viewed by your Lordship as lending additional weight to the considerations advanced by him in favour of a policy of abstention, on the part of the Treaty Powers, from extreme measures in the present unhappy condition of a part of Northern China.

LOFÊNGLUH

Rear-Admiral Bruce to Admiralty
(communicated by Admiralty, June 26)

(Telegraphic)   *Chefoo, June 26*, 1900

Commander Cradock, commanding British contingent, Tien-tsin relief, reports Tien-tsin communicated with and reinforced 23rd June. Commander-in-chief reported 10 miles from Tien-tsin, hampered by sick and wounded, and engaged with enemy.

Force landed: German 1,340; American 335; Russian Naval Brigade 235, troops 3,500; Japanese Naval Brigade 602, troops 1,050, expected 26th June 2,100; Austrians 26; Italian 138; French 421, 3 P.M. 25th June French expect one battery artillery, one battalion infantry.

Acting Consul-General Warren to the Marquess of Salisbury
(received June 27)

(Telegraphic)   *Shanghae, June 27*, 1900

Acting under instructions from the Viceroy, the Taotai of Shanghae asked the foreign Consuls to meet him yesterday in order to discuss the situation. He asked the Consuls at the meeting to telegraph to their respective Governments, suggesting that they should declare neutral all the districts other than those north of where fighting is actually in progress, and that if that were done they would then be able to guarantee the maintenance of order.

The allied Admirals' Proclamation, dated the 20th June, was the Consuls' reply. They declared that the foreign Powers were only fighting against the Boxers and those persons who opposed the forces sent to

Peking to rescue their countrymen there. That the duty of keeping the peace rested with the Chinese officials, and that they need have no apprehension of any attack on our part if no breach of peace or act of war was committed by China.

Consul Carles to the Marquess of Salisbury
(received June 27)

(Telegraphic)   *Tien-tsin, via Chefoo, June* 27, 1900
British column, under Major F. Morris, R.W.F., and Naval Brigade, under Commander Cradock, arrived at noon, 550 men strong; 1,500 Russians are reported to be at Tien-tsin Railway Station; 150 Americans and 50 Italians have also arrived 23rd June.

Consul Carles to the Marquess of Salisbury
(received June 27)

(Telegraphic)   *Tien-tsin, June* 27, 1900
Heavy firing has been heard for thirty-six hours north of Tien-tsin, where the Commander-in-chief is believed to be at a place named Pei-tsang, about 9 miles from here.

A note was received yesterday morning by the Commissioner of Imperial Customs from the Inspector-General, dated 19th June, 4 P.M., stating that the Legations had been ordered to leave Peking within twenty-four hours.

Sir C. Scott to the Marquess of Salisbury
(received June 27)

(Telegraphic)   *St. Peterburgh, June 27*, 1900

Count Lamsdorff has been at Peterhof with the Emperor all day, and early to-morrow morning he has to return there, but I have been able to communicate in writing to him the sense of your Lordship's telegrams of 25th June, and he promises that as soon as he is enabled to do so he will give me an immediate reply.

There is an utter absence of news at the Russian Foreign Office with regard to the present situation in and near Tien-tsin.

Sir E. Monson to the Marquess of Salisbury
(received June 27)

(Telegraphic)   *Paris, June 27*, 1900

M. Delcassé informs me that, beyond the two declarations he has already made in the Chamber, he has no statement to offer for the information of the Government of Japan in connection with the meeting of the foreign Representatives which the Japanese Minister for Foreign Affairs convoked at Tôkiô.

On the question of the co-operation of Japan on a large scale, his Excellency did not give me any intimation of his opinion.

On the whole, M. Delcassé's language was less optimistic than that which seems to have been held at St. Petersburgh to Her Majesty's Ambassador.

The Marquess of Salisbury to Acting
Consul-General Warren

(Telegraphic)   *Foreign Office, June* 27, 1900

Your telegram of to-day.

Your answer to the Taotai is approved.

The Marquess of Salisbury to Sir Chihchen Lofêngluh

Sir,   *Foreign Office, June* 27, 1900

I have the honour to acknowledge the receipt of your
note of yesterday's date, containing a telegram
received by you from his Excellency the Viceroy of
Huquang relative to the protection of foreigners and
native Christians residing in the Yang-tsze provinces.

I have to thank you for your action in the matter.

SALISBURY

Consul Carles to the Marquess of Salisbury
(*received June* 28)

(Telegraphic)   *Tien-tsin, viâ Chefoo, June* 24, 1900

News was brought yesterday by Bigham's servant,
who is quite trustworthy, of the Commander-in-
chief. He was being bombarded by a large number of
guns in a small arsenal called Wuku, north of Tien-
tsin, which he had seized. His losses were about 40
killed and 70 wounded, and relief was urgently
needed. Force to succour him leaves to-night.

Comparatively slight damage was done to the
foreign Settlements, which were shelled from the
18th to the 23rd June, except in the French
Concession, which suffered severely; the British

Consulate was also a good deal knocked about. The British casualties up to date of relief are 4 killed and 50 wounded, among the latter being 6 officers.

Admiralty to Rear-Admiral Bruce
(*communicated by Admiralty, June 28*)

(Telegraphic)   *June 28*, 1900

It is proposed to make Wei-hai Wei the base for troops in the north of China, and all ships containing stores will be directed to call at Hong Kong for orders.

Sir C. Scott to the Marquess of Salisbury
(*received June 28*)

(Telegraphic)   *St. Petersburgh, June 28*, 1900

Following official telegram from Admiral Alexieff, dated Port Arthur, the 26th June, published by Russian War Office this evening:

"On 24th June, General Stessel forced his entrance into Tien-tsin and effected junction with Anisimoff. Losses not great; details later."

Sir C. Scott to the Marquess of Salisbury
(*received June 28*)

(Telegraphic)   *St. Petersburgh, June 28*, 1900

Further official telegram from Admiral Alexieff, Port Arthur, 27th June. During night of 26th, detachment from Tien-tsin, commanded by Lieutenant-Colonel Shirinsky, and consisting of four Russian companies and similar number of foreigners, liberated Seymour detachment, escorting it to Tien-tsin; 200 of Seymour detachment wounded.

Sir C. Scott to the Marquess of Salisbury
(received June 28)

(Telegraphic)   *St. Petersburgh, June* 28, 1900

I communicated your Lordship's telegram of the 25th June to Lamsdorff, and have just received his Excellency's reply. The Russian Minister at Tôkiô has been instructed by telegraph to make the following reply to the Government of Japan:

"We can only highly appreciate the sentiments expressed by Japan in present circumstances, as also her view of Chinese affairs. We have no desire to hinder her liberty of action, particularly after her expression of a firm intention to conform her action to that of the other Powers.

"As regards Russia, her intentions have been clearly defined by the official communiqué published on the 24th instant.

"Admiral Alexieff has further received orders to regulate the measures which he might find necessary eventually to take in accordance with the developments in North China."

Acting Consul-General Warren to the Marquess of Salisbury
(received June 28)

(Telegraphic)   *Shanghae, June* 28, 1900

I have received the following telegram from Her Majesty's Consul at Chungking for transmission to your Lordship:

"In order to have a possible means of escape for the women and children, I have taken it upon myself to detain the British merchant-steamer "Pioneer" at

Chungking. A state of great anxiety prevails here owing to there being no gun-boat. I communicated with the Admiral by telegraph on the 19th June through the Consulate General at Shanghae, but I have not as yet received any reply. There are no means of communicating with Sir C. MacDonald. I am sending by mail a full report of what has been done."

Acting Consul-General Warren to the Marquess of Salisbury
(received June 28)

(Telegraphic)   *Shanghae, June* 28, 1900
I have received the following message from the Nanking Viceroy:

"I received the following Imperial Rescript on 25th June by telegraph:

" 'The Imperial Government continues as usual to accord every protection to the foreign Legations at Peking.' "

Mr Whitehead to the Marquess of Salisbury
(received June 28)

(Telegraphic)   *Tôkiô, June* 28, 1900
I have to-day been informed by Viscount Aoki that the division now mobilized would probably be very shortly embarked.

Viscount Aoki further stated that the communication, which in accordance with the instructions contained in your Lordship's telegram of the 22nd instant I made to the Japanese Government, was considered by them to be not so much a mere inquiry as a suggestion. It was possible for them to reply directly or indirectly, and they have chosen what seemed the preferable course by mobilizing their troops.

Consul Scott to the Marquess of Salisbury
(received June 28)

(Telegraphic)   *Canton, June* 28, 1900
I am informed by Li Hung-chang that he has received an Imperial Edict, by which he is commanded to remain in residence for the present, so as to ensure the preservation of order in the district.

The Marquess of Salisbury to Sir C. MacDonald
Sir,   *Foreign Office, June* 28, 1900
The Chinese Minister called on me to-day, and said that the Viceroy Li Hung-chang had requested him to inform me that the foreign Representatives at Peking were safe at Pei-tsang, a station on the Tien-tsin-Peking Railway, some 16 miles to the north of Tien-tsin.

SALISBURY

Count Lamsdorff to M. de Staal
(communicated by M. de Staal, June 29)
(Translation)

(Telegraphic)   *St. Petersburgh, June* 15 (28), 1900
We have been informed of the intention of Japan to take part in the re-establishment of order in China by Sir C. Scott and M. Isvolsky. The latter has been furnished with the following instructions in regard to the matter:

While appreciating the friendly sentiments which animate Japan, and which have suggested to Mr Aoki the overtures made by him to you, as well as the perfectly correct attitude adopted by that Power in view of the events which have occurred in China, we do not wish to hinder the liberty of action of the Tôkiô Cabinet, especially as the latter is quite disposed to act in harmony with the other Powers. As to the intentions of Russia, the Imperial Government has stated them in the recently published official communiqué.

Viscount Gough to the Marquess of Salisbury
(received June 29)

(Telegraphic)   *Berlin, June* 29, 1900
Dispatch of Japanese expedition to China.
Your telegram of 26th June.
The Minister for Foreign Affairs is absent with the Emperor, and the German Government has not yet given any answer.

Consul Carles to the Marquess of Salisbury
Tien-tsin, via Chefoo

(Telegraphic)   *June* 29, 1900
A message to the effect that the Legations are still in Peking has been received by a foreign Resident through the Customs Taotai.

Admiral Seymour's force, together with the relief force, arrived on the 26th instant. The casualty returns of the foreign detachments are incomplete; the British casualties are: killed, Captain Beyts and twenty-four men; wounded, seven officers and ninety-one men.

Vice-Admiral Sir E. Seymour to Admiralty
(*communicated by Admiralty, June* 29)

(Telegraphic)   *Chefoo, June* 29, 1900

Have returned Tien-tsin with force, unable to reach Peking by rail. On the 13th June two attacks on advanced guard made by Boxers, repulsed with considerable loss to Boxers, none our side. 14th June Boxers attacked train at Langfang in large numbers with great determination, but were repelled with loss of about 100 killed. Our loss, five Italians.

Same afternoon Boxers attacked British guard left to protect Lofa Station. Reinforcements were sent back and enemy driven off, 100 being killed—two of our seamen wounded. Guards pushed forward to Anting, engaged enemy 13th and 14th June, inflicting loss of 175—no casualties our side.

Extensive destruction of railway in our front having made further advance by rail impossible, it was decided, 16th June, to return to Yangtsun, where proposed to organize advance by river to Peking.

After my departure from Langfang two trains left to follow on were attacked 18th June by Boxers and Imperial troops from Peking, who lost 400 to 500 killed. Our casualties: six killed, 48 wounded. These trains joined me at Yangtsun same evening. Railway at Yangtsun found entirely demolished, and train immovable, forces short of provisions, and hampered with wounded, forcing us to withdraw on Tien-tsin, with which there had been no communication for six days, and supplies cut off 19th June, wounded and necessaries started by boats, forces marching alongside river.

Opposition experienced during whole course of river from nearly every village, rebels when defeated in one village retiring on next, and skilfully retarding advance by occupying well-selected positions, from which they had to be forced, often at point of bayonet, in face of galling fire difficult to locate.

23rd June made night march, arriving at daylight opposite Imperial Armoury, above Tien-tsin, where, after friendly advances, treacherous heavy fire was opened while men were exposed on opposite bank.

Enemy kept in check by rifle fire in front, while position was turned by party of marines and seamen under Major Johnstone, who rushed and occupied one of sallied points, seizing a gun.

Germans lower down silenced two guns, then crossed river, capturing them. Armoury then occupied by combined forces. Determined attempt to retake it made same and following days, unsuccessful. Found immense stores of guns, arms, ammunition, latest pattern.

Several guns mounted for our defence and shelled Chinese forts lower down—having found ammunition and rice could have held out some days, but being hampered by large number of wounded, sent to Tien-tsin to ask for relieving force, which arrived morning of 25th June. Armoury evacuated, and forces arrived Tien-tsin, 26th June. On leaving armoury destroyed it by fire.

Casualties to date:

	Killed	Wounded
British	27	97
American	4	25
French	1	10
German	12	62
Italian	5	3
Japanese	2	3
Austrian	1	1
Russian	10	27

Consul Carles to the Marquess of Salisbury
Tien-tsin, via Chefoo
(Telegraphic)   *June* 29, 1900
At a Consular meeting held to-day it was unanimously agreed to make the following suggestion to our respective Governments, viz, that the Chinese Government should be informed that in case the persons of the foreign Ministers are touched, the Mausolea of the dynasty will be destroyed by the European troops.

The Commander-in-chief gave his support to this decision on the 26th instant, and it is to be communicated to all the Admirals.

Consul Tratman to the Marquess of Salisbury
(*received June* 29)
(Telegraphic)   *Chefoo, June* 29, 1900
Nothing definite is known of Ministers, but they are supposed to be still in Peking. The damage done to

Tien-tsin has been exaggerated; English ladies are still there and likely to remain. Admiral Seymour has been relieved, and has returned to Tien-tsin with a loss of 62 killed and 212 wounded.

Acting Consul-General Warren to the Marquess of Salisbury
(received June 30)

(Telegraphic)   *Shanghae, June* 29, 1900

The following has been received from a reliable source, and the language of the Viceroy Liu and the Shanghae Taotai confirms its general terms:

"The Viceroy has received through the Governor of Shantung a Secret Decree dated the 20th June. This Decree, which is very curiously worded, is considered by the Chinese as the testamentary command of a dying Government. The Governors and Viceroys are ordered to protect the provinces under their administration, and to render assistance at the same time in the critical situation of affairs at Peking. The Chinese are of opinion that its language practically gives absolute authority to the Viceroys.

"A message has been received by Li Hung-chang from Jung-lu dated the 21st June, telling him to pay no further attention to Decrees from the capital. In combination with the Yang-tsze Viceroys, Li-Hung-chang has agreed no longer to recognize the Peking Government.

"A copy of the Secret Decree is in my possession. The language employed is non-committal, but I consider that Prince Tuan probably usurped the Imperial power about the 21st June. It is reported that Jung-lu is attempting to co-operate with the Chinese Viceroys and is opposed to him."

Admiralty to Foreign Office (received July 1)
Sir,   *Admiralty, July* 1, 1900
I am commanded by my Lords Commissioners of the Admiralty to transmit, for the information of the Secretary of State for Foreign Affairs, copy of a telegram, dated the 30th June, from Rear-Admiral Bruce, concerning the situation in China.

EVAN MACGREGOR

Enclosure

Rear-Admiral Bruce to Admiralty
(Telegraphic)   *Via Chefoo, June* 30, 1900
The conduct of Commander Stewart, "Algerine," and Commander Lanz, "Iltis" (German), at bombardment Taku forts was magnificent, and elicited admiration of allied ships.

River route to Tien-tsin, 51 miles from Taku, now open. Railhead now 9 miles from Tien-tsin, and road inwards not [now?] quite safe. Communication with Commander-in-chief, Tien-tsin, difficult. Force with Cradock had to fight way into Tien-tsin. Cradock also Commander storming party previously forts at Taku. Fort which commanded river 13 miles above Taku was found deserted by Lieutenant and Commander Keyes, and blown up by him, leaving passage up the river free. Keyes reports to-day arsenal Tien-tsin captured 27th June.

Naval brigade losses: five men killed. Lieutenant Colomb, "Endymion," slightly wounded; Gunner May and twenty-one men wounded. No further details. Warrender quite well, doing very good work, taking charge of all our forces on river and along lines of communication.

Vice-Admiral Alexieff, Governor-General of Port Arthur and Liaotung Province, Commander-in-chief of all Russian forces in the East, has just arrived on his way to Tien-tsin, taking supreme command of Russian forces. Captain Jellicoe shot through lung, doing very well.

Forces landed to date:

	Officers	Men
Germany	44	1,300
British	184	1,700
Austria	12	127
America	20	329
France	17	387
Italy	7	131
Japan	119	3,709
Russia	117	5,817
Total	520	13,500

With 53 field guns, 36 machine guns.

No details yet of killed and wounded with Commander-in-chief.

Viscount Gough to the Marquess of Salisbury
(received July 1)

(Telegraphic)   *Berlin, July* 1, 1900

With reference to your Lordship's telegram of the 26th June respecting the Japanese expedition, I have the honour to state that the German Government have sent me the following reply:

"No particulars ('modalitäten') of the proposed Japanese intervention are in their possession; they are unable to judge whether the interests of third Powers would be affected by it, or whether the responsibility of supporting it could be undertaken by Germany.

"Order can be restored in China, and the Empire's existence and the peace of the world be continued only by the maintenance of the accord which has hitherto existed among the Powers.

"Germany would therefore only take part in the steps which Her Majesty's Government have proposed, if, from the outset, she felt certain that the above-mentioned indispensable accord would not be thereby endangered."

I am sending by post to-night copy and translation of the reply of the German Government.

Acting Consul-General Warren to the Marquess of Salisbury
(received July 1)

(Telegraphic)   *Shanghae, July* 1, 1900

This morning news has been received here from Peking up to the 26th ultimo; all the power is in the usurper Tuan's hands and the situation is very grave. The Empress-Dowager and the Emperor are both in

Peking but powerless. Tung-fu-hsiang, the Mahommedan General with 15,000 well-drilled Kansu men and Tuan with Manchu troops, are determined to resist foreign troops. Jung-lu beseeches foreign Powers to rescue their subjects while there is time. Viceroys and Governors of all the southern and central provinces have united to resist the usurper and ask for assurance from Powers that the war shall not spread south however bad the situation at Peking may become. I have again given them assurances that Her Majesty's Government will not land troops except in the north while the Chinese authorities continue to maintain order. News has reached Shêng from Paoting-fu that German Minister has been murdered. I consider the position of foreigners in Peking extremely critical. They are said to have taken refuge at the British Legation.

Acting Consul-General Warren to the Marquess of Salisbury
(received July 1)

(Telegraphic)   *Shanghae, July* 1, 1900
I telegraphed to-day to Yuan-shih-Kai, Governor of Shantung, for the purpose of urging him to follow the example of the three great Viceroys in standing firm in the cause of order.

His reply is as follows:

"With regard to your telegram of to-day: My views are the same as those of the Viceroys. The rebels have reached Peking, have for a long time interrupted communication and have overrun the country. A messenger reached me on the 26th June with information that the foreign Representatives were still in the capital."

Vice-Admiral Sir E. Seymour to Admiralty
(communicated by Admiralty, July 1)

(Telegraphic)   *Chefoo, July* 1, 1900

Arsenal north-east of Tien-tsin Settlement captured the 27th June by combined forces. British engaged were Naval Brigade and 1st Chinese Regiment.

Consul Tratman to the Marquess of Salisbury
(received July 1)

(Telegraphic)   *Chefoo, July* 1, 1900

On the 13th June the German Minister at Peking was murdered by native troops. On the 23rd June there were only three Legations remaining. It is not stated which they were.

Lord Currie to the Marquess of Salisbury (received July 2)
Rome, June 28, 1900

I asked M. Visconti-Venosta to-day what steps the Italian Government intended to take with regard to events in China.

He said that they wished to take part in any concerted action that may be taken by the Powers for the protection of Europeans, and for the re-establishment of order. They could not contribute as largely to these ends as most of the other Powers interested in the Far East, but small contingents had already been landed from the Italian ships, and had acted with the international forces. There were at present only two Italian men-of-war in Chinese waters, but another was on its way, and two more would start in a few days, and would be provided with extra crews, so as to strengthen the ships already on the station and provide men for landing parties. Another vessel would be got ready with all dispatch. So that in a short time the Italian Squadron in Chinese waters would be composed of six vessels.

It was not decided to send any soldiers at present, as it was uncertain whether they would be required, but, in the event of circumstances making it desirable that Peking or any other point should be occupied by an international force, Italy would be ready to send a contingent to take part in such occupation, and would reserve her decision as to any larger force that might be eventually required.

It was impossible at present to judge how far the movement in China was likely to spread, and what efforts might be required to cope with it.

It was the wish of the Italian Government, M. Visconti-Venosta said, to co-operate with Great Britain and the other Powers, and he would be very glad to learn whether the course which they proposed to follow met with the concurrence and sympathy of Her Majesty's Government.

CURRIE

Viscount Gough to the Marquess of Salisbury
(received July 2)

Berlin, June 29, 1900

I have the honour to inform your Lordship that the Emperor has appointed Major-General von Hoepfner, Inspector of the Marine Infantry, to the command of the reinforcements which have been ordered to China. In the Imperial Order notifying this appointment it is directed that when the General arrives on the East Asiatic Station he is to place himself under the orders of the Commander of the Cruiser Squadron. In any land operations, however, General von Hoepfner is to assume the command of the forces employed.

I have the honour to transmit to your Lordship a translation of an Imperial Order, published in yesterday's papers, directing the formation of the expeditionary corps for China, and specifying the number of officers and men, etc., of which it is to consist.

GOUGH

Enclosure

Imperial Cabinet Order respecting the Formation of an Expeditionary Corps for China

(Translation) June 25, 1900

I command:

1. An expeditionary corps to be dispatched to China, is to be formed from my navy, consisting of the 1st and 2nd Marine Battalion, of a

horsed field battery, and of a detachment of Pioneers.

2. To the Commander of the expeditionary corps I grant the jurisdictional and disciplinary authority of a Commander of a division.

3. His Staff consists of—one Staff Officer as Chief of the Staff, one Captain, one Lieutenant, one Staff Surgeon, one Paymaster, one Evangelical and one Catholic Naval Chaplain, and the necessary subordinates.

4. A reserve battalion is to be formed as soon as possible in Kiel and in Wilhelmshaven for the 1st and 2nd Marine Battalion. Executory orders are issued by the Secretary of State for the Imperial Department of Marine.

5. The dispatch of and arrangements for transport devolve upon the North Sea Naval Station.

Kiel, on board my yacht "Hohenzollern."

WILLIAM

Admiralty to Foreign Office (received July 2)

Sir,   *July* 2, 1900

I am commanded by my Lords Commissioners of the Admiralty to transmit, for the information of the Secretary of State for Foreign Affairs, a copy of a telegram, dated the 1st July, from Rear-Admiral Bruce, relative to the crisis in China.

EVAN MACGREGOR

Enclosure

Rear-Admiral Bruce to Admiralty

(Telegraphic)   *Chefoo, July* 1, 1900

German Admiral reports Chinese runner, three days from Peking, arrived Tien-tsin yesterday; brought despatches to say all Europeans in great distress; situation desperate; hoping for relief every hour. German Minister has been murdered by Chinese regular troops, and large Chinese army advancing on Tien-tsin. Have had long conversation with Russian Governor-General. He agrees with me that, with all reinforcements expected, Russian and Japanese, it will only bring total to about 20,000 men, which would enable us to hold the base from Taku, Tien-tsin, and probably Pei-ta-ho, but impossible to advance beyond Tien-tsin.   4 P.M., 30th June.

Viscount Gough to the Marquess of Salisbury
(received July 2)

(Telegraphic)   *Berlin, July* 2, 1900

Count von Bülow left here for Wilhelmshafen in order to consult with the Emperor, upon receiving the official confirmation of the murder of the German Minister at Peking.

I was sent for this morning by Baron von Richthofen, who informed me as follows:

The German Consul at Tien-tsin has sent a telegram, dated the 29th June, in which it is stated that a Chinese messenger had arrived from Peking that day, bringing the following message, addressed to the Commander of the international forces, which had been dispatched by the Second Secretary in the German Legation, Herr von Bergen:

"Foreign community besieged in the Legations. Situation desperate. Hasten your coming. Sunday, 4 P.M.

"ROBERT HART"

The 24th June is assumed to be the date of the above message.

A further telegram has been received from the German Consul at Tien-tsin, stating that a second messenger, sent by a missionary, arrived on the 29th ultimo, having left Peking on the 25th. He reported that the military escorts of the Legations are suffering from want of ammunition, and he confirmed the murder of the German Minister and the burning of the majority of the Legations.

In view of the above information, and of that contained in Reuter's telegrams, the situation of all foreigners in Peking would appear to be most critical, if, indeed, they are still living. It is believed in the German Foreign Office that the foreign women and children, among them being the wife of the late German Minister, still remain in Peking.

Taking these facts into consideration, Baron von Richthofen then asked me, though he had not received any positive instructions from his Government to do so, whether Her Majesty's Government were prepared to propose any better measure, the effect of which would be immediate, than the one which the Consuls at Tien-tsin had proposed, namely, that a threat to destroy the Imperial tombs should be made, and whether to refuse a proposal which the best-informed persons on the spot had unanimously made, would not be to assume a great responsibility.

The Marquess of Salisbury to Viscount Gough
(Telegraphic)   *Foreign Office, July* 2, 1900
With reference to your telegram of the 2nd July respecting proposal of Consuls at Tien-tsin to threaten destruction of the Imperial Mausolea, you should inform Baron Richthofen that the proposal reaches us without any information as to the manner in which it is viewed by the Naval or Military Commanders on the spot.

We believe the Mausolea to be situated near Moukden and Hingking, in Manchuria, and it is probable that their destruction could only be effected by the dispatch of an expedition of considerable strength from Talienwan or Newchwang. The distance which would have to be covered would vary, according to the route and place of departure, from 100 to 200 miles.

We therefore feel unable to sanction a measure which would be so offensive to European opinion.

The threat appears, at first sight, very unlikely to have any effect upon mutinous soldiery or a riotous mob, and these are the factors which place the Legations in so perilous a situation.

Vice-Admiral Sir E. Seymour to Admiralty
(*communicated by Admiralty, July* 4)

Tien-tsin, June 30
(Telegraphic)   *via Chefoo, July* 3, 1900

Chinese couriers arrived from Peking with short message dated 24th June, stating that condition there desperate, and asking for help at once. Couriers interrogated state all Legations except British, French, German, and part of Russian destroyed. Europeans gathered in British Legation, have provisions, but ammunition scarce. One gate of city near Legation held by Europeans with guns captured from Chinese. Five of Marine Guard killed and one officer wounded; not much sickness at present. I propose to remain at Tien-tsin at present unless naval operations in Yangtsze or elsewhere. Vice-Admiral Alexieff is expected. Chinese inundated country near here yesterday from Grand Canal; object probably for defence of city to the south. No injury to us. General health good. All agreed that no advance on Peking possible for many days at least, owing to want of force and transport.

The Marquess of Salisbury to Mr Whitehead
(Telegraphic)   *Foreign Office, July* 4, 1900

Following just received from Admiral Seymour:
[*Repeats Admiral Seymour, 30th June, communicated by Admiralty 4th July.*]

This indicates a position of extreme gravity. You should communicate telegram at once to Japanese Ministers. Japan is the only Power which can send rapid reinforcements to Tien-tsin. No objection has been raised by any European Power to this course.

The Marquess of Salisbury to Mr Whitehead
(Telegraphic)   *Foreign Office, July* 6, 1900
Japan is the only Power which can act with any hope of success for the urgent purpose of saving the Legations, and, if they delay, heavy responsibility must rest with them. We are prepared to furnish any financial assistance which is necessary in addition to our forces already on the spot.

Her Majesty's Government wish to draw a sharp distinction between immediate operations which may be still in time to save the Legations and any ulterior operations which may be undertaken. We may leave to future consideration all questions as to the latter.

The Marquess of Salisbury to Mr Whitehead
(Telegraphic)   *Foreign Office, July* 6, 1900
Japanese troops for China: my telegram of to-day.
In the circumstances we are prepared to undertake this financial responsibility, since a fatal expenditure of time would result from international negotiations on the point.

Mr Whitehead to the Marquess of Salisbury
(received July 6)
(Telegraphic)   *Tôkiô, July* 6, 1900
I have just received a visit from the Japanese Minister for Foreign Affairs, who informs me that reinforce-

ments to make up the Japanese force to 20,000 men
will be sent as rapidly as possible.

The Marquess of Salisbury to Sir E. Monson
(Telegraphic)   *Foreign Office, July* 6, 1900
We have suggested to Japanese Government that they
should dispatch reinforcements to China as soon as
possible.

Inform French Government.

The Marquess of Salisbury to Sir C. Scott
(Telegraphic)   *Foreign Office, July* 6, 1900
The crisis in China.
You should inform Russian Government that Her
Majesty's Government have suggested to the Japanese
Government that they should, with as little delay as
possible, dispatch reinforcements to China.

Admiralty to Senior Naval Officer, Woosung
(communicated by Admiralty, July 6)
(Telegraphic)   *July* 6, 1900
Austro-Hungarian Government ask that Her
Majesty's ships may afford protection to Consulate
Shanghae, and, if necessary, receive staff on board.

You are to afford such protection as may be possible.

Sir C. MacDonald to the Marquess of Salisbury
(received July 9)
Peking, May 21, 1900
In my despatch of the 16th April I had to report to
your Lordship that in spite of the commencement of

a firmer attitude on the part of the Chinese Government towards the anti-Christian movement in North China, there still existed indications of danger in this neighbourhood from the "Boxer" Society.

The activity of the "Boxers" has showed no signs of diminution; reports of depredations in country districts indicated that armed bands of them were approaching daily nearer to Peking; while in the city itself the frequent spectacle of numbers of young lads practising in a kind of hypnotic frenzy, the peculiar gymnastic evolutions inculcated by the craft, and the appearance of numerous virulent anti-foreign placards posted in conspicuous places, combined to create considerable alarm amongst the native Christians of all denominations, a feeling which they were not slow in trying to communicate to their foreign spiritual directors.

I take this opportunity of enclosing a translation of one of these placards as a specimen of the silly superstitions which the leaders of this movement work on to further their designs. Several similar documents have been forwarded to this Legation, most of them less literary in composition, and containing more scurrilous abuse of foreigners, but all having for their theme the necessity of putting all foreigners to death. I have called the attention of the Yamên more than once to the posting of such placards, and have been assured that steps were being taken to put a stop to this dangerous practice.

Your Lordship will observe that, in Mgr. Favier's letter to M. Pichon [enclosed], the situation at Peking is painted in very dark colours. The Bishop declares that the conditions now are precisely similar to those preceding the Tien-tsin massacre of 1870, and asks that a guard of marines should be sent to protect the lives of French missionaries.

At the meeting of the Diplomatic Body which took place, accordingly, yesterday, the French Minister showed that he was profoundly impressed by the apprehensions of Mgr. Favier, and by reports which he had received from other sources. He expressed complete disbelief in the genuineness of the measures of which the Yamên had spoken to me, and declared that it was impossible to exaggerate the danger of the outlook.

Mgr. Favier has lived in Peking for over thirty years, and is in constant touch with Chinese of all classes, so that it was generally felt that, after making all due allowances for the colour which might have been lent to his words by the fears of his converts, his deliberately expressed opinion on the situation could not be treated with indifference. At the same time, we did not consider that the circumstances, so far as we were as yet in a position to judge, were such as to justify the bringing up of Legation Guards, and M. Pichon did not insist upon the immediate necessity for such a step. He produced the draft of a joint note which he proposed the doyen should be authorized to address to the Tsung-li Yamên, in which certain specific measures for the suppression of the "Boxers" were demanded, and, after some discussion, the terms of this note were accepted by the meeting.

As regards my own opinion as to the danger to which Europeans in Peking are exposed, I confess that little has come to my own knowledge to confirm the gloomy anticipations of the French Fathers. The demeanour of the inhabitants of the city continues to be quiet and civil towards foreigners, as far as my experience and that of my staff is concerned, although, from the undoubted panic which exists amongst the native Christians, it may be assumed that the latter are being subjected to threats of violence. I am convinced that a few days' heavy rainfall, to terminate the long-continued drought which has helped largely to excite unrest in the country districts, would do more to restore tranquillity than any measures which either the Chinese Government or foreign Governments could take. As this cannot be counted upon, my judgment as to the probability of continued security must be suspended until the Chinese Government shows by its action within the next few days, whether or not it has the will and the power to do its duty.

CLAUDE M. MACDONALD

Enclosure

PLACARD POSTED IN WEST CITY, PEKING

(Translation)   4*th moon,* 1*st day* (*April* 29, 1900)

In a certain street in Peking some worshippers of the I-ho Ch'üan ("Boxers") at midnight suddenly saw a spirit descend in their midst. The spirit was silent for a long time, and all the congregation fell upon their knees and prayed. Then a terrible voice was heard saying:

"I am none other than the Great Yü Ti (God of the unseen world) come down in person. Well knowing that ye are all of devout mind, I have just now descended to make known to you that these are times of trouble in the world, and that it is impossible to set aside the decrees of fate. Disturbances are to be dreaded from the foreign devils; everywhere they are starting Missions, erecting telegraphs, and building railways; they do not believe in the sacred doctrine, and they speak evil of the Gods. Their sins are numberless as the hairs of the head. Therefore am I wrath, and my thunders have pealed forth. By night and by day have I thought of these things. Should I command my Generals to come down to earth, even they would not have strength to change the course of fate. For this reason I have given forth my decree that I shall descend to earth at the head of all the saints and spirits, and that wherever the I-ho Ch'üan are gathered together, there shall the Gods be in the midst of them. I have also to made known to all the righteous in the three worlds that they must be of one mind, and all practise the cult of the I-ho Ch'üan, that so the wrath of heaven may be appeased.

"So soon as the practice of the I-ho Ch'üan has been brought to perfection—wait for three times three or nine times nine, nine times nine or three times three*—then shall the devils meet their doom.

* Meaning obscure.

The will of heaven is that the telegraph wires be first cut, then the railways torn up, and then shall the foreign devils be decapitated. In that day shall the hour of their calamities come. The time for rain to fall is yet afar off, and all on account of the devils.

"I hereby make known these commands to all you righteous folk, that ye may strive with one accord to exterminate all foreign devils, and so turn aside the wrath of heaven. This shall be accounted unto you for well doing; and on the day when it is done, the wind and rain shall be according to your desire.

"Therefore I expressly command you make this known in every place."

This I saw with my own eyes, and therefore I make bold to take my pen and write what happened. They who believe it shall have merit; they who do not believe it shall have guilt. The wrath of the spirit was because of the destruction of the Temple of Yü Ti. He sees that the men of the I-ho Ch'üan are devout worshippers and pray to him.

If my tidings are false, may I be destroyed by the five thunderbolts.

Enclosure
Père Favier to M. Pichon

(Translation)

Apostolic Mission of Peking and North Chih-li, Peking, May 19, 1900

The situation becomes daily more and more serious and threatening. In the Prefecture of Paoting-fu more than seventy Christians have been massacred, three other neophytes have been cut to pieces. Several villages have been looted and burnt, a great number of others have been completely deserted. Over 2,000 Christians are fugitives, being without food, clothes, or shelter; in Peking alone about 400 refugees—men, women, and children—have already been given shelter by us and the Sisters of Charity; in another week's time we shall probably have several thousands to look after; we shall be obliged to disband the schools, colleges, and all the hospitals, to make room for these unfortunate people. On the east pillage and incendiarism are imminent; we receive more and more alarming news every hour. Peking is surrounded on all sides; the Boxers are daily approaching the capital, being only delayed by their measures for exterminating all Christians.

I beg you will be assured, M. le Ministre, that I am well informed and am making no statements at random. The religious persecution is only a blind, the main object is to exterminate the Europeans, and this object is clearly indicated and written on the Boxers' standards.

Their accomplices in Peking are awaiting them; they are to begin by an attack on the churches, and are finally to assault the Legations. For us, indeed, here at Pei-t'ang, the day of attack has actually been fixed; the whole town knows it, everybody is talking about it, and the popular excitement is clearly manifest. Last night, again, forty-three poor women, with their children, flying from massacre, arrived at the Sisters' Home; over 500 people accompanied them, telling them that, although they had succeeded in escaping once, they would soon all perish here with the rest.

I will not speak of the numberless placards, M. le Ministre, which are posted in the town against Europeans in general; new notices appear daily, each more clearly expressed than the last.

People who were present at the massacres in Tien-tsin thirty years ago are struck by the similarity of the situation then with that of to-day; there are the same placards, the same threats, the same notices, and the same want of foresight. Then also, as to-day, the missionaries wrote and begged, foreseeing the horrible awakening.

In these circumstances, M. le Ministre, I think it is my duty to request you to send us, at least to Pei-t'ang, forty or fifty sailors, to protect us and our belongings. This has been done on much less critical occasions, and I trust you will favourably consider my humble supplication.

ALPH. FAVIER

Sir Chihchen Lofêngluh to the Marquess of Salisbury
(received July 12)
Chinese Legation, London
July 11, 1900

I have the honour to forward your Lordship the enclosed translation and Chinese text of a telegram from the Emperor of China to Her Majesty the Queen-Empress, and to request that you will have the goodness to have them presented at their high destination as soon as possible.

LOFÊNGLUH

Enclosure

The Emperor of China to Her Majesty the Queen
(Translation)
(Telegraphic)   *Peking, July* 3, 1900
The Emperor of China to Her Majesty the Queen of England, Empress of India, sendeth Greetings:

Since the opening of commercial intercourse between foreign nations and China, the aspirations of Great Britain have always been after commercial extension, and not territorial aggrandizement.

Recently, dissensions having arisen between the Christians and the people of Chihli and Shantung, certain evilly disposed persons availed themselves of the occasion to make disturbances, and these having extended so rapidly, the Treaty Powers, suspecting that the rioters might have been encouraged by the Imperial Government, attacked and captured the Taku forts. The sufferings arising from this act of hostility have been great, and the situation has been much involved.

In consideration of the facts that of the foreign commerce of China more than 70 per cent belongs to England, that the Chinese Tariff is lower than that of any other country, and that the restrictions on it are fewer. British merchants have during the last few decades maintained relations with Chinese merchants at the ports as harmonious as if they had both been members of the same family. But now complications have arisen, mutual distrust has been engendered, and the situation having thus changed for the worse, it is felt that, if China cannot be supported in maintaining her position, foreign nations, looking on so large and populous a country, so rich in natural resources, might be tempted to exploit or despoil it; and, perhaps, differ amongst themselves with respect to their conflicting interests.

It is evident that this would create a state of matters which would not be advantageous to Great Britain, a country which views commerce as her greatest interest.

China is now engaged in raising men and means to cope with these eventualities, but she feels that if left to herself she might be unequal to the occasion should it ever arrive, and therefore turns to England in the hope of procuring her good offices in bringing about a settlement of the difficulties which have arisen with the other Treaty Powers.

The Emperor makes this frank exposure of what is nearest to his heart, and hopes that this appeal to Her Majesty the Queen-Empress may be graciously taken into her consideration, and an answer vouchsafed to it at the earliest possible moment.

Mr Whitehead to the Marquess of Salisbury
(received July 12)

(Telegraphic) *Tôkiô, July* 12, 1900

I have informed Admiral Seymour by telegraph that Lieutenant-General Teranchi, second in the General

Staff, is being sent by Japanese Government to discuss with him and Admiral Alexieff a scheme of combined operations.

Chinese Imperial Edict (communicated by Sir Chihchen Lofêngluh, July 13)

Translation of an Imperial Edict dated Peking the 29th June, received by the Privy Council, and by the Board of War forwarded to the Provincial Treasurer of Chihli for transmission to the Chinese Ministers residing at the various Courts in Europe, America, and Japan, through the Taotai of Shanghae.

In view of the circumstance that the Treaty Powers have unexpectedly assembled considerable forces in China, it is expedient that the Chinese Ministers accredited to foreign countries should be made acquainted with the situation of affairs at present, and the causes that have led to it.

We therefore command that the following account of what has recently taken place in Peking be communicated to them, in order that they may the better be the interpreters of our intentions with respect to the Treaty Powers.

The present unsatisfactory state of affairs originated in the formation of a Society consisting of disorderly persons in the provinces of Chihli and Shantung. The ostensible object of the Society was the practice of athletics, attended by strange rites founded on the pretended possession by its members of supernatural powers.

At first the authorities, viewing it as harmless, took no notice of the Society or sect with any measures for its suppression, but soon, spreading like wildfire, branches of it were found everywhere, and in the matter of a month great numbers of its adherents were found even in Peking, where they were considered as a mystical sect to which crafty and designing persons introduced anti-Christian proclivities.

About the 10th June its enmity towards Christianity was no longer a matter of doubt. In spite of every effort to control them, they then set fire to some of the missionary buildings in Peking, and at the same time killed some of the native Christians.

When things began to assume a serious aspect, the foreign Representatives in Peking requested permission to bring up some soldiers for the protection of the Legations, and, the situation appearing critical, this was agreed to, and the Legation guards were accordingly increased by the number of about 500 men of the different nationalities. This is an evidence of the desire of the Chinese Government to maintain friendly relations with foreign Powers.

On other occasions, when foreign soldiers had been called up to Peking for the protection of the Legations, the men were confined to the premises of the several diplomatic establishments, so no collision ever occurred between them and the populace, but on this occasion, no sooner had they arrived than they were sent with their arms to patrol the streets, and sometimes they used their arms to fire on the people. Nor did they seem to be kept under proper control, but were allowed to roam, apparently at their own will, wherever they liked; some of them having been stopped in an attempt to enter the Tung Hwa mên, a gate leading to the Imperial Palace, by which entrance is strictly forbidden. These acts on the part of the foreign soldiers so incensed the people that, lending ear to the false rumours that were being industriously disseminated amongst them by members of the Society, many of the people joined the latter, and, setting the law at defiance, proceeded to assist them in murdering the Christians and committing other outrages.

At this point the foreign Representatives called for more troops, but the advance of the reinforcements that were sent having been opposed by the combined forces of the Shantung and Chihli rebels, they have not, as yet, succeeded in reaching Peking.

It was not from any reluctance on the part of the Imperial Government that they did not adopt stronger measures for the suppression of the Boxer movement as soon as its real object became evident, but because of the danger to which, in the meantime, the Legations and Europeans in the disturbed districts would have been exposed. It was necessary to temporize, in order that the Society should not be provoked into attacking the Legations and committing further acts of hostility towards the Christians whilst the Imperial Government were preparing to deal an effectual blow. Any failure to do this at the first blow, might have led to the perpetration by the

Boxers of acts which the Imperial Government would have viewed as a national calamity.

It was in view of these considerations that the Imperial Government thought of the expedient of requesting the Diplomatic Body to temporarily absent themselves from Peking, and it was whilst this project was being debated by the Tsung-li Yumên that Baron von Ketteler, the German Minister, was killed whilst on his way to the Yamên. On the previous day he had written to the Yamên asking for an appointment, but in consequence of the menacing attitude of the populace who then thronged the streets, it was not considered safe for him to be seen outside of the Legation. The Yamên, therefore, declined his request for an interview. The wisdom of this course was seen in the lamentable result of his attempting to come to the Yamên the next day. The increasing audacity of the crowd now then knew no bounds. It was now too late to send the foreign Ministers to Tien-tsin under the protection of a sufficient well-armed escort as the Yamên had intended doing; so, the only other course open to the Yamên was to continue the Ministers in Peking under the protection of an adequate guard of Chinese troops. And this was done, the officer in command of the guard having stringent orders to protect the Legations effectively in every possible emergency.

On the 16th June the officer in command of the allied fleets at Taku, much to our surprise, demanded of General Lo Yung Kwang the surrender of the forts under his command, at the same time informing him that, in case of non-compliance, they would be attacked and taken at 2 o'clock next day. It was the duty of Lo Yung Kwang to hold the forts, so he had no alternative but to refuse the demand.

At the appointed time the allied Commander opened fire on the forts and eventually captured them.

These hostilities were not of China's seeking. No false estimate of her power led her to measure her forces with those of the combined fleets. She fought because she could not do otherwise than resist.

This point the Ministers must make unmistakably clear to the respective Governments to whom they are severally accredited. They will also take occasion to explain to the different foreign Secretaries the action of the Chinese Government and the motives by which it was actuated under the ever-changing circumstances which have led to the present complicated state of our foreign relations.

Orders of a very imperative character have been given to the officer charged with the protection of the foreign Legations to exert himself to the utmost in order that nothing untoward may happen to them.

Our Ministers are to remain at their respective posts in foreign countries, and to continue to discharge their official duties with unremitting care and assiduity.

Let this be transmitted to them.

Respect this.

PART TWO

∞⋙◈⋘∞

SIR CLAUDE MACDONALD'S DIARY
OF THE SIEGE, 20 TH JUNE TO
14 TH AUGUST, 1900

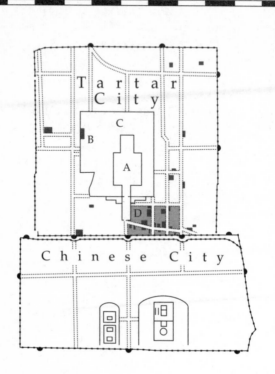

•••••• Brick walls
⬛ Gates
⋯⋯⋯ Streets

A. The Forbidden City
B. Pei T'ang Cathedral
C. The Imperial City
D. Legation Quarter in 1900

EVENTS UP TO AND INCLUDING 20TH JUNE

Before the 20th June, barricades, but not of a very substantial nature, had been erected across the road which runs between the Imperial Maritime Customs compound and the Austrian Legation, in front of the Italian Legation in Legation Street, facing east. This was composed mainly of upturned Peking carts, and was to meet any attack from the east, whilst against an enemy advancing along the street from the west, one

Legation Quarter, Peking, in 1900

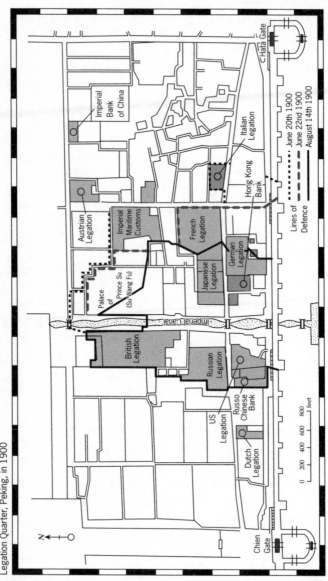

had been put up between the Russian and American entrance gates.

The British marines held the North Bridge over the canal with a picket; the other detachments also patrolled the roads in the vicinity of their Legations and pickets were stationed at various points.

The German detachment had made a barricade in the street between their Legation and the Tartar city wall facing east, and the Americans one at the back of their Legation facing west.

Immediately the death of the German Minister became known, it was clear that we had a different foe to deal with, and preparations were made to defend the Legations in grave earnest.

A plan which had been sketched out previously by the commandants of the Legation guards was immediately put into execution; all barricades were hastily strengthened and outlying pickets withdrawn. All women and children were ordered into the British Legation. This order was pretty generally carried out, only a very few remaining at the Peking Hôtel, situated in Legation Street. More than 100 women and children came in during the afternoon, for all of whom accommodation had to be found. This does not include some 600 to 700 Chinese Christians, servants, converts, etc., of whom more than half were women and children.

The student interpreters gave up their quarters and slept in the "tingerhs," or open reception halls; most of the staff also gave up their houses. The Second Secretary's (Mr Dering's) was handed over to the Russian Legation and bank. The Accountant's was handed over to the members of the French Legation and their wives and families. The ladies of the American Legation occupied the doctor's quarters, and one block of the students' rooms was given over to the Imperial Maritime Customs. Fifteen ladies were accommodated in the ball-room of the Minister's house, twelve others lived in the smoking-room, two families occupied the billiard-room, whilst many missionaries slept in the corridors. The Belgian, Japanese, and Italian Ministers and their families, together with the widowed Baroness Ketteler, were also accommodated in the Minister's house. In all, 78 Europeans slept in this building, which usually accommodated a dozen; whilst nearly 900 lived within the four walls of the Legation during the eight weeks' siege, the normal number being about sixty.

The whole day [June 20] was occupied in bringing in and storing provisions and making further arrangements for the defence. Punctually at 4 P.M. the Imperial troops opened fire from the north and east, mostly on the Austrian and Italian barricades, and then commenced the organized attack on the Peking Legations by the forces of the Chinese Government.

So far as the Boxers were concerned, the garrisons of the various Legations could have routed their entire force in Peking, for the *bona fide* Boxer believed implicitly in his supernatural powers, and disdained to use a fire-arm; but, with Mauser and Mannlicher bullets humming through the air, we knew that a different order of things had begun. Captain Strouts withdrew the picket from the North, or Yu Ho Bridge, to a barricade which we had erected at the main gate of the Legation; the enemy, from the roofs of houses, opened fire on this barricade, and the fire was at once returned. The removal of this picket was in accordance with the plan decided upon by the military authorities; it was in a very exposed position, useful against Boxers, but untenable against rifle fire.

Across the canal, which runs from the Imperial city past the main gate of the Legation, is situated the Su Wang Fu, or Palace of Prince Su, a direct descendant of one of the Ironcapped Princes. This Prince had been friendly and helpful, allowing part of his Fu enclosure to be used as a shelter for the Christian refugees. I had, on this account, had some communication with him through a Mr Hubert James, a professor at the Peking University, one of the refugees in the Legation. When the firing commenced, Mr James informed me that Prince Su seemed very much distressed at hostilities having broken out, and asked him to convey a message to me, stating that he was convinced that if he could carry the Court an assurance that the foreign Powers had no intention of partitioning the Empire, orders would be given for a cessation of the attack. I authorized Mr James to say that the mission of all the foreign Representatives in Peking was to maintain friendly relations with the Chinese Government and that Great Britain, and so far as I knew, none of the other Powers had any designs whatsoever on the integrity of the Chinese Empire.

Mr James departed with my message and returned shortly afterwards saying that he had delivered it to the Prince, who had immediately mounted his horse and galloped off in the direction of the Palace. Mr James returned to the Fu; suddenly, to the consternation of the small detachment holding our barricade at the main gate, he was seen to run out on the North Bridge, which at that time was swept by the enemy's fire and our own; instantly three Chinese cavalry soldiers charged the unfortunate man and with blows of their sabres drove him before them off the bridge; he was not actually seen to fall, but there is no doubt that he was then and there cut down. A hurried volley was fired at the cavalry, but owing to the failing light it was impossible to see with what result. Mr James, who spoke Chinese well, had without doubt left the north gate of the Fu and proceeded on to the bridge to expostulate with the soldiery, but orders had evidently now been given to kill all foreigners at sight, orders which Tung fu Hsiang's men were only too ready to obey.

The attack now became fairly general and if pressed home must have been attended with disastrous results for, as I have stated, none of the Legations had at that time been put into a thorough state of defence. Desultory attacks took place during the night, all of which were repulsed. On the following day work was continued on the barricades and the provisioning of the British Legation was proceeded with.

21ST JUNE

The Austrian Legation was vigorously attacked; a French marine was killed and an Austrian wounded behind the Austrian barricade; this led to the Austrians falling back on the French Legation, thereby exposing the entire east side of the large block of Customs buildings, which up to this had been held by volunteers belonging to the Maritime Customs. Before long, immense volumes of smoke arose, and the roar of flames and crash of falling timbers were heard, denoting that the Chinese had not been slow in taking advantage of this retirement. The incendiarism continued, and during the day the Austrian and Dutch Legations were burnt, as well as the greater part of the Customs quarter and the Chinese Bank. The enemy were particularly bold in their attacks, exposing themselves freely, and suffering in proportion; it was noticed that nothing fanned their failing courage so much as a conflagration. From the French and German Legations it was reported that some troops, presumably Prince Ching's, were seen to open a heavy fire on the Boxers in the neighbourhood of the Hata Gate. Meanwhile, Tung-fu Hsiang's troops, noticeable by their uniforms—red, with black velvet facings, the cavalry having on their breast three characters denoting "the cavalry of Kansu"—were very busy in their attacks on us from the north and west.

At 9 A.M. a determined onslaught was made on the Students' Mess, a two-storeyed building overlooking the Imperial Carriage Park; the upper storey of this building, which formed the library, had been barricaded, and was held by a garrison of marines and volunteers. The enemy were driven off, leaving six of their number, making picturesque dots of colour in the long grass. German marines reported that Prince Ching's troops had entered into conversation with them on the wall; these troops said that they had orders to prevent any Boxers coming on the wall of the city, and Prince Ching had issued the strictest injunctions to shoot any Boxers doing so; they added that foreign soldiers could come up there as much as they pleased.

All day the garrison not actually engaged in repelling the attacks of the enemy were busy in assisting the organization of the defence within the British Legation; a Committee of Public Comfort was appointed, the members consisting of representatives of the various Legations, the Maritime Customs, and the various missionary bodies. Various Sub-Committees were also appointed, one of the most important being the Fortification Committee, under the Rev. F.D. Gamewell, of the American Methodist Mission; this Committee, under its intelligent and energetic Head, subsequently rendered the most invaluable services; the Food Supply Committee, to look after and regulate the stores and supply of food; the Water Committee, in charge of the five wells in the Legation, to measure each day the depth of water and regulate its consumption; the Committee on Native Labour, a most important one, very ably presided over by the Rev. W. Hobart, an American missionary; by the proper management and organization of native refugees splendid results were obtained. There was, of course, some little confusion at first, but before many days everything worked smoothly, and by applying to the proper Committee even watches could be mended and boots repaired free of charge.

22ND JUNE

In the forenoon it was reported to me that, owing to a mistaken order, the garrisons of the various Legations were all falling back on the British Legation, and on going to the main gate I found this to be the case.

Fortunately, the Chinese were not aware of the critical state of affairs, or, at any rate, did not take advantage of it. Before it was too late the matter was rectified, and the various marine detachments marched back to their respective Legations, the Germans, however, losing two men in so doing.

While this was going on, a certain amount of confusion naturally prevailed, as a result of which the Russian, French, and Italian Ministers begged me, as having some previous military experience, to take general command of the defence of all the Legations, and I accepted the task. I subsequently saw the American and Japanese Ministers, who confirmed the above request. I would take this opportunity of stating that during the remainder of the siege I was throughout supported with the greatest loyalty and willingness by my colleagues, and also by the Commanders of the various detachments. I would also beg to acknowledge the splendid assistance given to the defence in general, and myself in particular, by the missionaries, especially the Americans, to whose powers of organization the comfort and comparative safety of the British Legation were mainly due.

The Italians, who, previous to their enforced retirement, had gallantly, by a bayonet charge, repulsed an attack of the enemy, found, on returning, that their Legation was in flames. Their Commander immediately reinforced the nearest post, which was the German, and together with their detachment held a barricade on the city wall above the German Legation, and also one in the street below. By my direction the Italians subsequently occupied, together with the Japanese, the Su Wang Fu. This Palace or Fu subsequently formed one of the principal parts of the defence; it consisted of an enclosure of some 12 to 14 acres, surrounded by walls 20 feet high. Inside were some thirty buildings of various sizes, beautiful gardens, houses, pavilions, rockeries, summer-houses, etc.

The garrison of the Fu now consisted of the Japanese detachment of one officer and twenty-three men, besides nineteen volunteers, most of whom had served in the army; the Italian detachment of one officer and twenty-eight men, the whole under the command of Lieutenant-Colonel Shiba, Japanese Military Attaché; also twelve British marines and the same number of volunteers, mostly from the Maritime Customs, a small garrison to hold so extensive a post. This was the weak point of the entire defence, the garrison being altogether too few in numbers for the area defended; it was, however, under the circumstances, unavoidable, as it would have been impossible to have surrendered any single point of the defence without seriously endangering the rest.

A general glance at the position held may here be useful.

The garrison were fighting practically with their "backs against a wall," in this instance the wall being that of the Tartar city, 50 or 60 feet high, and 30 feet wide at the top.

The German and American Legations were the two which abutted on to this wall, a narrow street only dividing them from it. The line of defence on the 21st June commenced on the east at the German Legation, and, crossing Legation Street, took in the French Legation, a compound of 5 or 6 acres, containing the Minister's residence and those of his staff.

The line then followed the wall of, and included, the Su Wang Fu; from there it crossed the canal, and took in the British Legation going south. It included the Russian and American Legations, finishing again at a point on the wall some 500 yards from where it commenced.

In the defence the French Legation formed a sort of salient, open to close attack from the north and east, and also from the city wall and houses to the south-east. By the burning of the Customs quarter the Su Wang Fu, generally called the "Fu," became open to attack from the east; its north wall faced the enemy, its west side was covered by the British Legation.

On the south of the Fu were situated the Spanish and Japanese Legations, which were included inside the lines of defence and never suffered from a direct attack. The British Legation was completely open to attack from the north and west; abutting the north face were the buildings, temples, examination halls, and library, of the world-renowned Hanlin Yuan or Hanlin College, commonly called "The Hanlin." On the west was the Imperial Carriage Park, consisting of an enclosure 12 acres in extent, with handsome trees and capacious storehouses tiled with Imperial yellow, in which were stored the Imperial chairs and carriages.

This Carriage Park was held throughout the siege by the enemy; it was noticeable that the yellow-tiled roofs of the store-houses, though they commanded the British Legation at close range, were never utilized by the enemy; to the south of the Carriage Park, and abutting the west wall of the Legation, in some places actually built against this wall, were the houses which surrounded an open space some 2 acres in extent, which went by the name of the Mongol Market; as its name implied, this enclosure was used by the Mongols, who visit Peking in the winter, as a market-place for their wares.

The south of the Legation was defended from direct attack by the Russian Legation, but between these two, which are some 50 yards apart, was a large collection of Chinese and Mongol houses. These houses were a source of grave danger to both Legations, on account of the ease with which they could be set on fire. South of the British Legation was situated the Russian, the north-east half of which was protected from direct attack by the British, but the north-west formed part of the Mongol Market, and was under fire from the north and west; abutting the west of this Legation were Chinese houses, the whole of the south wall faced Legation Street, on the opposite side of which was the American Legation, which was separated from the Tartar city wall by a narrow street. It was commanded at close range from the wall.

At the commencement of the siege the west of the American Legation was protected by the Russian Bank, which for some few days was held by Russian and American marines and volunteers. It was evident from the commencement that to the general defence the most important points were the Tartar city wall and the Fu, the former because an enemy holding it commanded easily the entire circle of defence, and the Fu, because its loss would render the British Legation almost untenable, and here were assembled, by the decision of the Military Commandants, the women and children, spare ammunition and provisions, also; an enemy holding the Fu would menace the retreat of the German and French Legations. The wisdom of the above-mentioned decision on the part of the Commandants was amply borne out by subsequent events.

Late in the afternoon the enemy developed their attack from the west, opening fire from the Mongol Market, the houses surrounding which had been loopholed. A private of the marines was shot dead on the west wall of the Legation whilst returning the enemy's fire. Two 9-pr. Krupps also opened fire from the Chien Gate of the city, doing damage to the Russian Bank and American Legation.

The buildings in the Hanlin College were, from a military point of view, a source of great danger to the British Legation, owing to the possibility of their being set on fire, and it was proposed to destroy them. As the buildings were, however, of a very substantial nature, it would have been difficult to do this without explosives, of which we had none; to set them on fire would have been the best course, but one attended with very great danger to ourselves. One could only hope, therefore, that the Chinese, a nation of *literati*, would hesitate to commit this act of vandalism and destroy their national library. By way of precaution, however, a hole was made through the wall which separated us from the Hanlin enclosure, and a search party sent out under Captain Poole; the various buildings were found unoccupied by the enemy, neither were any signs of preparation for setting them on fire visible.

23RD JUNE

Communication with the Russian Legation was established through a hole in the South Wall, and the work of destroying the shops and small buildings situated between the two Legations was commenced; this was a most important necessity in order to establish safe communication between the two Legations, and to ward off all danger from incendiarism; the enemy kept up a heavy rifle fire on the working party, some of whom were wounded, including

Mr Peachy, a student interpreter, but considerable progress was made.

A brisk fire was now commenced and kept up by the enemy from some high roofs belonging to the recently established Electric Light Company, as also from the adjoining premises of the Chinese Colonial Office; these buildings lie some 300 yards to the north-east of the British Legation; the Italian quick-firing 1-inch gun was brought up and together with our sharpshooters from the north stable picket returned the fire with telling effect. This Italian quickfirer was by far the most useful of the machine-guns brought by the various detachments. The others were an Austrian Maxim, a British five-barrelled Nordenfelt, very old pattern; and an American Colt automatic. Unfortunately, there were only 150 rounds brought up with the Italian gun. In the course of the siege the entire gun detachment of this quickfirer, consisting of five men, were either killed or wounded.

At 11.15 A.M a determined attack was made on the Hanlin enclosure. It was preceded by a sharp infantry fire from the Imperial Carriage Park; the greater part of the Hanlin was then set on fire by the enemy; the fire bell rang and all hands were soon at work endeavouring to extinguish the flames; the Chinese had carefully selected their day and had evidently no qualms whatever as to the vandalism they were committing; a fresh north wind was blowing and the flames were carried nearer and nearer to the Legation buildings; a stubborn fight was maintained until late in the afternoon when the flames were got under, but not before more than three-quarters of the temples, examination halls, and libraries, forming the Hanlin College, had been destroyed. There remained only one building entirely intact, the heavy wooden eaves of which overshadowed and almost touched the students' quarters in the Legation; had these caught fire, the Legation would most probably have been doomed, but owing to the splendid efforts of the garrison, men, women, and even children, joining in the work of passing water to the engines, as well as to a providential change of the wind to another quarter, the danger was averted. Orders were given to save as many of the valuable books in the Hanlin as possible; the greater part had, however, been destroyed either by fire or water; a good many were taken away as mementoes by members of the garrison.

The enemy pursued these incendiary tactics at other parts of the defence, and at 3 P.M. a fire was reported from the Russian Legation, but M. de Giers reported that he thought he could cope with it with the resources at his command. Late in the afternoon the American detachment reported a determined attempt to set fire to their Legation buildings. I sent over immediately a reinforcement of twenty-five men and some members of the fire brigade. The Russo-Chinese Bank next to the American Legation was on fire, and partially burnt down, but the Legation escaped. For the next five days the enemy endeavoured to burn out the garrison, and a daily and hourly fight took place, resulting in a complete victory for the defenders.

The practice from the enemy's Krupp 9-pr. battery on the Chien Gate now became very accurate, and for a time they paid particular attention to the national standards flying over the entrance gates of the Russian and American Legations. The American flag-staff was shot away,* and a considerable hole made in the gate-way. The Russian flag had also some narrow escapes, and they were both eventually removed to places where they could not be seen from the wall. This battery also shelled the barricade on the wall at the back of the American Legation, bursting two shells in the barricade itself, the range being about 800 yards. Unfortunately we had no artillery heavy enough to silence these guns, and our riflemen were so scattered it was all we could do to keep in check those of the enemy. The 9-pr. which was to have accompanied the Russian detachment had most unfortunately been left behind on the platform of the railway station at Tien-tsin, though the ammunition had been brought.

*N.B. Sir C. MacDonald telegraphed on the 29th January, 1901, to the effect that this incident took place not on the 23rd June, but later, on the 6th July.

24TH JUNE

Early on this morning an attack was made on the American and Russian Legations, resulting in some casualties on our side. A determined attack was also made on the Fu, the Chinese trying to breach the high wall on the north-east corner, but were driven off with loss. They also effected a lodgment on the Tartar city wall immediately behind the American Legation, where they displayed their banners, and seemed to be waiting for orders to fire. A brilliant charge along the top of the wall by a small force of Germans and Americans, led by the intrepid Lieutenant von Soden, put the enemy to flight, and the pursuit was kept up almost to the Chien Gate. Here the pursuing party had to retire, finding themselves face to face with a Chinese barricade. In this gallant affair the enemy lost from eight to ten killed and three banners.

While this was going on the British Legation was attacked in a determined manner from the Mongol Market, the attack being directed against the south stable quarters, the enemy working their way through the Chinese houses up to the wall of the Legation. They then set fire to part of the stables, and threw stones and other missiles into the stable-yard. A sortie was instantly decided upon, a hole was made in the wall, and a party of marines headed by Captain Halliday dashed into the burning buildings, and cleared them at the point of the bayonet. Unfortunately Captain Halliday was almost immediately wounded very severely by a rifle-shot through the shoulder and lung, and had to give up the command. Notwithstanding the severe nature of his wound, Captain Halliday shot three of his assailants, and, refusing all aid, walked to the hospital, a distance of some 200 yards. I regret to say, owing to the severity of the wound, the services of this excellent officer were lost to the defence for the rest of the siege.

Captain Strouts now took command of the sortie, and inflicted considerable loss on the enemy, killing thirty-four in one house. One marine was mortally wounded, and others slightly in this affair, which had a most excellent effect, as it destroyed some 200 yards of cover which the enemy possessed, and drove them back to their barricades situated at the same distance from the Legation wall.

During the morning an equally brilliant sortie was made by Colonel Shiba from the north-east corner of the Fu at the head of ten French, ten Italians, and ten Japanese marines, and some British and Japanese volunteers, driving the enemy out of and past the Customs buildings. In the meanwhile the American detachment under Captain Myers had effected a lodgment on the Tartar wall, and a barricade had been commenced, a special gang of coolies to work on it being told off under an American missionary. By the following morning this barricade was completed. Unfortunately it was constructed at the head of the east ramp leading up to a bastion, thus leaving the bastion and the west ramp to be taken possession of by the enemy should they be so minded. The ramp leading up to the barricade was under fire from the Hata Gate, and many casualties occurred in going up to it. I myself saw three "converts" shot on the ramp in the space of five minutes. The enemy maintained a smart fire on this position, as also on the barricades across the street below. The fire on the wall was so severe that any casualties which occurred could not be attended to until nightfall, and the dead had to remain where they fell.

The French and German Legations had meanwhile been keeping up a stubborn defence. The

Germans held a barricade facing the Hata Gate, on the wall, and also on the road between the Legation and the foot of the ramp, and the French a barricade across Legation Street looking east. As evening closed in a British marine was dangerously wounded whilst walking inside our Legation compound. At the time he was shot down several ladies and children were within a few yards. It is a noticeable fact that during the entire siege only three casualties took place in the actual grounds as distinguished from the defences of the Legation. A marine was shot dead coming out of the guard-room by a bullet which skimmed the roof of the constables' quarters; the third casualty was a lady seriously wounded on the tennis lawn.

25TH JUNE

During the night and early morning the barricades on the wall and in the street at the back of the American Legation were badly damaged by shell fire from the Chien Gate; ten Germans and ten British marines were sent to reinforce, two British marines were almost immediately wounded by shell fire, one of whom subsequently died.

French reinforcements, together with Customs and Legation volunteers, under Captain Poole, were sent to the Fu, which was hard pressed; in this attack one French marine and two Japanese were killed and two Italians wounded.

Shortly after 4 P.M. great excitement was caused in the British Legation by the appearance of a small group of men carrying a board on the North Bridge, and word was passed to the northern defences and to the Fu to cease fire. By means of glasses from the north stable the board was made out to be an Imperial Decree stating that the Chinese troops were sent to protect the Legations and stop the firing, and adding that a despatch would be handed to the Legations on the North Bridge. One of the garrison, a Chinaman, volunteered to go out and receive the despatch; he was furnished with a notice board with black characters painted thereon, to the effect that the Imperial Decree had been understood, and that the despatch would be received; wearing an official hat the messenger sallied out watched by an expectant garrison; on arrival at the bridge he was received with cries of "Lai, la" ("He has come"), whereupon his courage seemed to fail him, and dropping the board he retreated hurriedly back to the Legation, arriving unhurt.

Two Mandarins accompanied by soldiers appeared round the corner of the bridge and everybody hoped that communications with the enemy were about to be opened, but some dropping shots were heard and the Mandarins and soldiers quickly disappeared. It was thought at the time that some too zealous sentries in the Fu had been unable to resist

the temptation of shooting a Mandarin, and had disobeyed orders; but I have subsequently ascertained
that the shots were fired by Tung fu Hsiang's soldiers
at the party bearing the Imperial Decree, and that one
of the bearers was actually shot dead, the rest taking
to flight. The board with the Imperial Decree
inscribed thereon remained for many days on the
bridge, a curious commentary on the thousands of
bullets which swept over it and pattered on the roofs
and defences of the Legations.

The immediate effect, however, of this notice was
a sounding of horns in the Imperial city, which was
taken up all round the defences and the firing immediately ceased, thus showing very clearly the complete
command the *de facto* Government, whether
Dowager-Empress, Prince Tuan, or both had over the
troops. The lull in the firing was the signal for
increased activity in the British Legation on the part
of Mr Gamewell and his Fortification Committee,
and soon some hundred of converts were busily at
work strengthening weak places and adding to the
defences. Our advanced posts in the Hanlin entered
into conversation with the Chinese soldiers; from the
latter it was gathered that Yung Lu had ordered the
"cease fire," and that a communication was coming
from him to us, but it never came.

Previous to the appearance of the board, the
Germans and Americans had been hotly engaged,
and the Italian gun had been sent to the wall barricade to endeavour to keep down the shell fire from
the Chien Gate, but had itself been put out of

action, both gunners having been seriously wounded and carried to the International Hospital. By 8 P.M. the firing had altogether ceased; shortly after a few shots were exchanged between the French in their Legation and the opposing barricades; a few desultory shots were also fired on the wall. On this day the Chinese took to building barricades of a more substantial nature and scientific design; up till now they had fired from barricades hastily constructed, from roofs of houses, and from behind ruined walls, and must have suffered severely.

About midnight, Prince Tuan and the war party having presumably again got the upper hand a tremendous fusilade was opened from all sides, but principally from north and north-west. This was the heaviest fire to which we had yet been subjected, and the bullets struck and ricochetted off the roofs of the various buildings like hailstones; this fire was kept up all through the night, and very few of the garrison obtained any sleep. The Americans were badly pressed in the barricade below the wall and reinforcements were called for from the French Legation, but Captain D'Arcy was unable to send them, his own post being hotly attacked; ten British marines were accordingly sent as soon as they could be spared.

26TH JUNE

In the morning the enemy, exhausted evidently by their efforts of the previous night, kept fairly quiet, allowing the worn-out garrison to snatch a few hours sleep. At 9.30 desultory sniping took place all round the defences.

Mr Cockburn, Chinese Secretary, and Mr Ker, Assistant Chinese Secretary, remained with the picket in the north stables the whole day, in case any message should come from the Imperial city, but in vain, and it was now evident that the war party was in the ascendant, and that a policy of extermination of the Legations had been decided on. The enforced retreat of Admiral Seymour and the successful blockade and bombardment of Tien-tsin, of which we were, of course, unaware, would be sufficient to account for this decision.

Today was organized the last reserve, and the following order was posted on the Bell Tower:

> In case of heavy firing, all men with guns of any description who are not on special duty at the time are to assemble at once at the Bell Tower and there await the orders of Captain Strouts.

Subsequent instructions were given that the assembly should only take place at the ringing of the "general attack bell."

The French Legation was severely attacked towards evening, and heavy volleys were fired into it from the enemy's barricades.

27TH JUNE

This promised to be a lively day. The firing became very heavy all round as early as 2 A.M. At 8 A.M. the firing slackened somewhat; but a smart attack was made on the Fu, and Colonel Shiba sent for the Italian gun. Fresh gunners having been procured, the gun was sent to him.

At 2.30 the American Legation called for reinforcements, and a reserve of five British marines, which were now always kept ready at the main gate, were immediately dispatched with a promise of ten more, if necessary. Ten British marines were already in the American barricade; this made twenty-one British marines, rather more than one-third of the available force, on duty outside the British Legation.

At 4 P.M. a heavy fusilade commenced on all sides, and the bugle sounded to general quarters. There was also heavy firing from the north-east corner of the Fu, and a Japanese orderly came hurriedly over with a note for me from Colonel Shiba. It ran thus:

> Dear Sir, They are nearing to break down the Fu's wall. I want to crush them when they come in. Will you please send some more reinforcements to me with the bearer.

Five marines and five volunteers were immediately sent. Shortly afterwards Colonel Shiba came over and reported that the enemy, having breached a hole in the north-east corner of the wall, had poured through into the Fu. He was, however, prepared for this incursion, and opened a murderous fire on them from surrounding loop-holes. The enemy fled in panic, trampling each other down in their efforts to escape through the hole by which they had entered, and leaving over twenty of their dead in the enclosure.

To cover their retreat they set fire to a temple at the corner of the Fu, and for the rest of the afternoon occupied themselves in dragging their dead through the hole in the wall by means of long poles with hooks attached to the ends.

At 8 P.M. the American detachment reported that 200 Boxers, compelled by Chinese soldiers to advance, had attacked the street barricade, but had been forced to retire with a loss of fifty killed. This number is, I think, somewhat excessive.

At 10.30 the "general attack" bell was sounded. The reserves turned out smartly and in very creditable numbers. The firing ceased shortly after 11, and a fairly quiet night ensued.

28TH JUNE

The enemy had evidently constructed gun platforms during the night for their two Krupp guns
in the Fu, and with these they devoted themselves
to bombarding the north wall at close range (about
10 yards) in order to breach the wall further. They
also turned their attention to the "Hôtel de
Pékin." The upper storey of this building was
struck twenty-six times by shell, without, however,
doing any harm to the occupants, who were in the

lower storey. The ruins of the Russo-Chinese Bank were occupied this day by the enemy.

At 6.30 P.M. the "general attack" bell was again sounded. The enemy had manned their loophole in the Mongol Market; and opened a heavy musketry fire against the stable quarters. Suddenly a gate at the north-west corner of the market flew open, and two Krupp guns opened fire at the top story of the stable quarters at a range of about 200 yards. Shell after shell crashed into the building, completely wrecking one window, shattering the barricades of the next, and driving the defenders out of the two upper rooms down below into the stable yard. Our men were not slow to return the fire, but having been driven out of the top storey of the building we could only bring a few rifles to bear. These, however, delivered an effective fire into the gateway, where, through the smoke, we could see the gunners at work. These, however, stuck to their guns, and it was only when it seemed as if the upper storey of the house must come down, that the fire suddenly ceased.

Experts say that two or three more rounds and the supporting walls would have given way, sending the heavy Chinese roof crashing into the storey below. The Chinese gunners must have suffered severely, for they were considerably exposed, and they never again attempted an artillery attack upon the Mongol Market.

The food supply suffered considerably during this bombardment, two mules and a pony having been killed by exploding shells. Several of the men had narrow escapes, but only two were wounded.

The wall behind the American Legation and the Legation itself were hotly attacked during the day. Mr Conger, writing from his Legation, says:

> Besides the attack of last evening our people on the wall and in the street below had two heavy attacks during the night. This morning they can be seen in largely increased numbers; they have occupied the inclined ramp opposite ours, and have planted a banner near the top, within 100 yards of our position, but we cannot touch them. If they attack, Captain Myers can repulse them, if not in great numbers. I have instructed him to hold on to the last minute, and am sure he will.

The enemy did not leave their barricade, but contented themselves with a continuous fusillade from their loopholes.

29TH JUNE

Two sorties had been arranged for this morning: one under Captain Wray and one under Captain Poole. The former consisted of 26 British, 10 Russians, 5 French, and 5 Italians, and the latter, of 5 marines and 10 volunteers. Captain Wray's party attacked the Mongol Market with a view, if possible, of capturing the two Krupp guns which had done such damage the day before; the guns had, however, been removed, and the sortie retired, setting fire to some houses; there were no casualties.

This sortie would have effected more, but so many nationalities were represented on one spot that orders given were not understood and some confusion resulted. Captain Poole's party penetrated into the Carriage Park, but were brought up by a high barricade; when near the same they came under a heavy cross-fire at close range, and had to retreat, fortunately without any casualties, though the fire was very hot, the bullets pattering like hail all round the hole in the wall through which the retreat had to be effected.

During the forenoon the enemy's artillery at the north-east corner of the Fu was particularly energetic; the gunnery, however, was erratic, several of the shells coming over the Legation, and finding a home in the Chinese city south of the Tartar wall. Reinforcements were sent into the Fu, 5 marines and 5 volunteers. Shortly after 10 the Chinese set fire to a large pavilion at the north-east corner of the Fu, and effected a lodgment in the grounds. They crept up under cover of ruins, etc., with long poles, at the end of which tow dipped in kerosene was tied. With these they set fire to the heavy overhanging wooden eaves of the Chinese buildings, which were very old, and burnt like tinder. It was only by being burnt out that the plucky defenders were forced to fall back.

Dr Lippett, surgeon of the American detachment, was dangerously wounded whilst talking to his Minister.

Captain D'Arcy, the gallant defender of the French Legation, was severely attacked and sent for reinforcements: 5 British marines, 5 volunteers, and 10 Japanese were immediately sent and assisted in repelling this attack. The British detachment was cheered by their French comrades when leaving the Legation.

Lieutenant Herbert, second in command of the French detachment, was killed whilst directing the defence, and two French marines were brought in wounded to the International Hospital, which had been established in this Legation under Drs Poole and Velde, surgeons of the British and German Legations respectively.

This had been a bad day for the defence: every single nationality had to deplore the loss of some of its members, and the French and Japanese, after hard fighting, had lost ground.

It had always been supposed that heavy rain would have the effect of driving the Chinese under shelter, and that a rainstorm while it lasted would result in quiet times for us. At 10 P.M. heavy rain commenced, and was the immediate signal for a most tremendous fusillade that quite surpassed anything that had ever taken place before. There was little or no artillery fire, but the roar, for it can be called by no other name, of musketry continued without intermission until daylight. There was no necessity to ring the alarm bell, for the entire garrison stood to arms during the whole night, thinking that this waste of ammunition must be the precursor of something more serious. Nothing, however, happened, and the damage done, except to trees and roofs, which were badly cut about, was practically nil. To maintain so continuous a fire I am of opinion that the Imperial regiments must have relieved each other in the firing line. The vast majority of the hail of bullets were going very high, and again the Chinese city must have suffered seriously. At a low computation 200,000 rounds must have been fired by the Chinese during the night.

30TH JUNE

Up till 9 A.M. the enemy remained quiet, having without doubt passed a sleepless night, but shortly after 9 they showed in large numbers opposite the German posts and, in reply to a communication from the German Chargé d'Affaires, a reinforcement of ten British marines was sent to assist in repelling the attack; two of this reinforcement were soon carried back severely wounded by splinters from shells; one has since died. Fighting had now become severe, and three German marines were killed and two wounded, but the enemy were repulsed having suffered heavily; the French, also, though attacked and hard pressed, drove off their assailants with loss.

At 11 P.M. the picket in the south stable reported what looked like a search-light far away on the southern horizon. I watched the light in question for some time; it certainly had the appearance of a search-light, or rather lighthouse, low down on the horizon; its resemblance to a search-light, however, was not sufficiently pronounced to warrant a notice being put up on the Bell Tower, where all events of interest were posted.

1ST JULY

This morning began quietly, but at 9 A.M. the enemy, notwithstanding their lessons of the previous day, showed in force towards the Hata Gate, and creeping up in the ramps surprised the German guard of ten men, under a non-commissioned officer, who retired down the reverse ramp, thereby exposing the rear of the American barricade some 450 yards distant; the latter coming under a reverse fire also left the wall, and the situation for a time was very critical; the

Chinese, however, did not realize or at any rate did not avail themselves of the advantage they had gained: Russian reinforcements were at once sent to the Americans, and shortly afterwards they reoccupied their barricades, but the German barricades on the wall remained in the hands of the enemy until the end of the siege.

At 10.30 a further reinforcement consisting of ten marines, under Captain Wray, was sent to relieve Captain Myers on the wall; seven marines also went to the German Legation; whilst this was going on a fierce attack was made on the French Legation; Mr Wagner, one of the Customs volunteers, was shot dead and the garrison momentarily fell back to their last line of defence, leaving the German Legation in a somewhat exposed and critical position. M. von Below, German Chargé d'Affaires, sent word to me informing me of the state of affairs and asking for reinforcements; though the Kansu troops were busy attacking our north and north-west defences, Captain Strouts was able to detach six men and a corporal to the relief; the French had in the meanwhile advanced and reoccupied their Legation.

The enemy had during the night built formidable barricades in the north of the Carriage Park; to cope with this the Italian quickfirer was with some difficulty hauled up into the Students' Library, a large upper storey room, and opened with deadly effect on the said barricade, completely silencing its fire.

At 2 P.M. Captain Wray who, it will be remembered, had been sent to Captain Myers' assistance on the wall, was brought in with a Mauser bullet through the shoulder. I had given this officer orders whilst on the wall to commence a barricade some 200 yards east of the American one in order to hold the enemy in check from the Hata Gate side and to cover the rear of the Russo-American position. On advancing towards the spot indicated he and his party were met by a severe cross-fire from both the Hata Gate and Chien Gate, the Mauser bullets from the latter just clearing the top of the American barricade in rear of the little party, and ricochetting along the wall, they nevertheless continued to construct the work. Captain Wray, whilst directing his men, was wounded soon after; one of his party was also shot down. The fire now became so hot that it was quite impossible to continue the work; Captain Wray, therefore, ordered a retreat, which was carried cut with most exemplary coolness under a severe fire.

At 3.15, Lieutenant Paolini, the officer commanding the Italian detachment in the Fu, reported that the Krupp gun, which had been firing all day, had been moved nearer, and he thought, by making a sortie, he might be able to take it; he asked for assistance, and also for permission to make the attempt. Thinking the proposition rather risky, I consulted Colonel Shiba, in whose judgment of affairs in the Fu I had the fullest confidence.

Colonel Shiba replied that he thought the capture of the gun practicable, and that the sortie should be made. I accordingly gave orders that the desired reinforcements should be sent to Lieutenant Paolini, and that he might proceed. There was no time to discuss the details of the sortie, as the position taken up by this gun was evidently only temporary, but the general idea was for Lieutenant Paolini's party to attack from the west, while Colonel Shiba attacked from the east. The reinforcements detached by Captain Strouts consisted of seven British marines and five volunteers, the latter all student interpreters in the Consular service. I ordered all firing to cease from the north stable picket and main gate, and waited results.

The attacking party sallied out of the gate of the Fu, and going along the wall, disappeared round the corner, up a lane which forms the north boundary of the Fu. A heavy fusillade was heard, and a marine was seen staggering back, waving his hand as if to attract attention; he had not gone very far when he fell. Three of the garrison instantly dashed out and brought him in. No man of the attacking party returned, and it was hoped that the attack had proved successful; this, however, proved subsequently not to be the case. Lieutenant Paolini was severely wounded, two Italian marines killed, and seven marines wounded, two of the latter being British. Mr Townsend, one of the student interpreters, was also severely wounded. It appeared that when the party turned into the lane they were met by a severe fire from a barricade some forty yards in front, as well as from the left wall of the lane, which was only some 18 to 20 feet broad. Lieutenant Paolini was shot almost immediately, whilst gallantly leading the party;

two Italian marines also fell, one shot dead, the other mortally wounded (he died almost at once). The barricade in front, some 8 feet high, was a blaze of fire, as well as the side wall.

The little party, finding themselves in a death trap, sought to escape through a hole or breach in the wall of the Fu, which was, however, only large enough to allow of two passing through at a time; it was whilst getting through this breach that two other men were wounded. Mr Russell, a young student interpreter, with great presence of mind, ordered his party of four volunteers to take cover behind a small heap of earth and bricks, and wait till the regulars had got through the hole. As soon as all had passed through, the students dashed across the lane one at a time; it was in doing this that Mr Townsend was shot in the shoulder and thigh, and fell. He was, however, pulled through the hole, still retaining possession of his rifle. Mr Bristow, another of the party, with great coolness and presence of mind, picked up and brought in the rifle belonging to the Italian marine, whose dead body was lying in the lane. But for Mr Russell's cool action, the confusion and consequent loss amongst the attacking party would most certainly have been greater.

A fight now took place over the dead body of the marine, but the fire was so deadly in the lane it was found impossible to recover it; three of the enemy, tempted, doubtless, by the reward offered by the Chinese Government for the head of a foreigner, came out from behind their defences, but were instantly shot down by the north stable picket from an advanced post on the other side of the canal.

Lieutenant-Colonel Shiba came over to me at once and reported the ill-success of the sortie, for which he very generously took the entire blame.

It was impossible to reconnoitre the ground outside our defences, so that sorties were at all times very risky, and, with so small a garrison, only to be undertaken under very special circumstances. Colonel Shiba's party had also encountered an unexpected barricade, and been forced to retire. Had we been able to capture the enemy's gun and its ammunition, the loss we suffered would have been small in comparison to the addition to our strength in the shape of even one piece of artillery. Lieutenant Paolini's wound was found to be severe, and he was detained in hospital; his place was immediately taken by Mr Caetani, Secretary of the Italian Legation, an ex-officer of Italian cavalry.

The evening passed fairly quietly. At 10:30 the light I have alluded to was again reported. I went, together with the signalman of Her Majesty's ship "Orlando," to the upper storey of the First Secretary's house, and the light was plainly visible; the signalman said it was evidently a flash-light. As it might possibly belong to the force which was on its way (we hoped) to relieve us, and by way of cheering up the spirits of the garrison, the following Notice was posted up the next day on the Bell Tower:

Last night, between 10 P.M. and 2 A.M., an electric flash-light was seen on the south-eastern horizon; its approximate distance from Peking, 25 miles. The flashes were regular, and occurred at intervals of almost a second, with a pause of between five to ten seconds between forty or fifty flashes.

2ND JULY

Gangs of coolies were at work all night on the American barricades on the Tartar city wall, and some excellent work was put in, the barricades being very considerably strengthened. Spies coming in to Colonel Shiba stated that troops were being withdrawn from Peking towards the south. These statements were received with caution.

Up till 10 o'clock, however, very little firing took place, and it seemed as if the enemy were either withdrawing part of their force or engaged in making fresh plans for attack. At 10:30 the Krupp guns opened fire on the Fu, and an occasional shot took effect on the defences; the majority, however, were going high. During the forenoon the enemy commenced to construct a large barricade in front of the main gate of the Hanlin, about 60 yards from our northern barricades. A few well-placed shells from the invaluable Italian quickfirer, which had again been hauled up to the Students' Library, demoralized their working party, and they did not continue.

Various important defences were commenced to-day in the British Legation. It was evident that the enemy were concentrating their attack on the Fu, either because they knew how important a point it was in the defence, or because they were aware from their spies that the buildings immediately to the south of it had been allocated to the converts, and it was against these latter that the Chinese seemed especially incensed. Should the Fu fall into the hands of the enemy, the British Legation would be completely commanded by its west wall, and the enemy would be able to bring up their Krupp guns to within 40 yards of the east wall of the British Legation and batter it down, in the same way as they had done to the north wall of the Fu. By my orders the Fortification Committee, under Mr Gamewell, commenced to strengthen the east defences; the wall itself was furnished with a doubled row of loopholes and thickened to a breadth of 10 ft, so as to render it proof against artillery, and traverses were erected to protect the western defences from reverse fire.

At 9 P.M. the American Minister and Mr Squiers, his Secretary of Legation, both of whom had seen military service, and whose experience was invaluable to the defence, came over to report that the Chinese had advanced across the bastion in front of the Russo–American barricade on the wall under cover of a species of sap or stone wall, and had erected a tower at the end of the sap, from which they could actually throw stones at the defenders of our barricade, from which the tower was only distant some 25 feet. They pointed out that it was absolutely necessary to take this tower and the Chinese barricade by assault, to prevent the enemy rushing our position on the wall, which was in imminent danger.

I immediately fell in with their views, and promised a reinforcement of fifteen men, which, with the ten marines already on duty, made up a total of twenty-five; with them went Mr Nigel Oliphant, who volunteered for the sortie. The attacking party, under Captain Myers, United States' Army, collected behind the wall barricade at 1:30 A.M. on the 3rd July; the party consisted of Captain Myers and fourteen American marines, a Russian officer, Captain Vroubleffsky, and fifteen Russian marines, Mr Nigel Oliphant and twenty-five British marines. No marine officer was available, two, Captains Halliday and Wray, being in hospital wounded, and Captain Strouts could not be spared from the British defences.

Captain Myers addressed the men in a short speech, pointing out clearly the plan of attack: the Anglo-American detachment, under his immediate command, was to attack the tower, follow along the sap, and then assault the barricade on its left or southern side; the Russian detachment was to attack the Chinese barricade on the right or northern end, where it abutted on to the top of the ramp.

At a given signal the whole party swarmed over the American barricade; the night was very dark and threatening rain. The English and Americans, with Captain Myers at their head, entered the tower, which they found unoccupied. They followed along the sap. Here Captain Myers received a severe spear wound in the knee and was disabled. At the south end of their barricade the Chinese had left a small lane or opening to connect with the sap. Through this the Anglo-American party streamed and engaged the enemy, hand to hand, Mr Oliphant shooting two with his revolver. A small encampment of tents was found behind their barricade. The enemy was cleared out of these, and driven down the ramp, leaving twenty-five of their dead on the wall.

The Russians, gallantly led by Captain Vroubleffsky, had in the meanwhile climbed over the right of the barricade and joined in the combat.

The enemy's position, including the whole bastion, was now in our hands, and work was commenced to strengthen what we had taken. A tremendous musketry fire was opened on the working party from a second barricade some 60 yards further along the wall, severely wounding a non-commissioned officer of marines. Just before dawn heavy rain came on which lasted several hours and caused great discomfort to the men. Our losses were two American marines killed and Captain Myers wounded; one Russian killed and two wounded; and three British marines wounded, all severely.

The above was one of the most successful operations of the siege, as it rendered our position on the wall, which had been precarious, comparatively strong. Work was continued day and night, and every opportunity taken to improve the advantage gained. At dawn the Krupp guns again began pounding away at the Fu defences, which were severely knocked about, and several casualties took place. The rain which had set in at dawn continued until sunset; the canal which separated the British, American, and Russian Legations from the remainder of the defence came down in flood, and threatened to carry away the covered way and barricade which had been constructed across it; as soon as the water subsided, which it fortunately did next morning, work was started, and a culvert to carry off the water was constructed.

The heavy rain had an excellent effect from a sanitary point of view, as it helped to clear out the canal, which from the number of decaying bodies of horses, mules, and dogs, which had been killed in or near the same by the wild fire of the enemy, had become very offensive and insanitary; but it played havoc with the earthworks and defences generally, and the fortification gangs were hard at work repairing damages. The enemy's works were also much impaired, and they lost heavily when repairing them.

During the afternoon the halyard of the Union Jack flying over the British Legation gatehouse was cut by a bullet and the flag came down with a run. Attempts were made to rehoist it by the signalman and armourer of Her Majesty's ship "Orlando," but the fire on the top of the gate-house was too hot; the flagstaff was let down to the ground through the tower, the flag nailed to the staff and then rehoisted into its old place. Amongst the small crowd of bystanders who helped with a will to hoist the heavy staff were the Representatives of three of the Great Powers.

At 9 P.M. heavy firing began against the Russian Legation and our new position on the wall, resulting in a few casualties. One of the enemy crept up in the dark to the Russian barricade and thrust a spear through one of the loopholes, narrowly missing a Russian sailor. The owner of the spear was instantly fired at from the neighbouring loopholes, but owing to the darkness it was impossible to see with what result. The flash-light was again seen, but clearer and with more movement. It was particularly bright at 2 A.M.

At my request a Return was furnished to me this day by the various officers commanding the detachments of the number of casualties which had taken place since the 20th June. They were as follows:

British marines: 2 killed, 15 wounded, including 2 officers.

Bluejackets, Italian: 5 killed, 7 wounded,
1 officer.
Bluejackets, Russian: 3 killed, 11 wounded.
Bluejackets, Japanese: 5 killed, 11 wounded.
German marines: 8 killed, 7 wounded.
Bluejackets, French: 6 killed, including 1 officer,
5 wounded.
Bluejackets, Austrian: 3 killed, 3 wounded.
American marines: 6 killed, 6 wounded, 1 officer.

All the wounds were severe and necessitated removal
to hospital. Total, thirty-eight killed and fifty-five
wounded.

4TH JULY

This being the anniversary of American Independence, the Anglo-Saxon community amongst the
besieged had decided that the relieving force would
appear to-day; knowing the difficulties of transport I
did not share in their anticipations, though when
appealed to, I did my best to encourage their hopes.
Several attempts had been made through the converts to communicate with the outside world, from
whom we had received no news whatever since the

commencement of the siege. Our messengers were at first let down over the Tartar city wall or went through the canal sluice gate under the same. None had succeeded, so far as we knew, in piercing the strict cordon, drawn round us; some had returned baffled in their efforts; and some we feared had been killed.

To-day a Shantung lad of about 14, well known to the American missionaries, volunteered to go; he took a letter from me to the British Consul sewed up in a piece of oil-cloth; the package was flat, just an inch long and half-an-inch broad; instead of concealing it in the thick sole of his shoe or sewing it into his clothes, hiding places with which the enemy had become well acquainted, he concealed it in a bowl of rice which he carried with him, after the fashion of some Chinese mendicants. As this was the first of our messengers who got through, his adventures are worth recounting.

He left the water gate at night, and after having narrowly escaped capture, reached the south gate of the Chinese city; watching his opportunity he slipped through with some mendicants and gained the open country, working his way with great caution from village to village. As he was not certain of the road to Tien-tsin, and fearing to excite suspicion by making inquiries, he used, on arrival at a village, to join the children at play and from them ascertain by degrees the general lie of the country, the names of adjoining villages, and the direction of Tien-tsin. The country was overrun with Boxers, and the villages were full of wounded, the result of the fighting with Admiral Seymour. When within sight of Tien-tsin he was commandeered by the enemy and made to work for them for over a week; at last he managed to escape and slipping through the allied sentries, which was undoubtedly the most risky part of the journey, he arrived at Tien-tsin on the 19th, five days after the taking of the Chinese city by the allies. He wandered about for a couple of days before he met any European who could talk Chinese, but at last he was fortunate enough to do so and was at once taken to the British Consul, where he delivered his letter on the 21st instant, which, though dated the 4th, was the latest news received from Peking. He started back on the 22nd and made the return journey in six days.

The lad stated that when he arrived in the vicinity of Tien-tsin the enemy were in the greatest state of demoralization, flying in every direction and leaving their artillery in ditches and hidden in the millet fields. On the return journey he noticed that, finding they were not pursued, they had recovered most of their guns and were entrenching themselves at Pei-tsang and other places. All the above we ascertained on the 28th instant, when the lad returned.

The letter which was received on the 21st by the British Consul was the *facsimile* of several others I had sent on previous occasions, the number of casualties only being altered from day to day. On this day, the 4th July, we had forty-six killed, including civilians, and about double that number severely wounded; of these, eight civilians had been killed and eleven wounded. The slightly wounded were not entered in the Returns and only went to hospital to have their wounds dressed and then returned to duty. The letter gave the relieving force, for of course we always counted on a relieving force, all needful information with regard to the position we held, and also pointed out that the water or sluice gate through the Tartar city wall afforded the easiest means of entering the Legation quarter.

5TH JULY

At a European shop within our lines were found some Japanese fireworks. The light-hearted Japanese garrison amused themselves at night by a pyrotechnic display, but one of their number discovered that a very effective missile might be constructed by opening these fireworks and filling them with nails, scrap iron, etc.; this was accordingly done and used against the Chinese with considerable effect.

The upper storey of the "Hôtel de Pékin" was again severely knocked about by the enemy's shells from the Chien Gate; the Secretary's quarters in the German Legation were rendered untenable from the same cause. The enemy were during the morning very active in the Hanlin. A party under Captain Poole were out clearing the ruins, when the fire became very severe and a retreat was ordered. Mr David Oliphant, of my Consular staff, was busy cutting down a tree in company with the signalman of the "Orlando," and before he had time to obey the order, was shot through the body and fell; the signalman stayed behind him under a shower of bullets until a stretcher was brought. The wound was mortal and the poor young fellow died and was buried the same afternoon; his loss was deeply felt by the whole British community, with whom he was an immense favourite; owing to his coolness under fire, and his knack of commanding men, I had appointed him in charge of the eastern defences of the Legation and I felt his loss very keenly.

At midday the sentries in the upper storey of the Students' Library and quarters reported the enemy at work amongst the yellow tiles on the top of the Imperial city wall, which is distant some 200 yards from the north wall of the Legation. At first it seemed as if they were loopholing it for musketry, but by means of field-glasses through the foliage of the trees two guns could plainly be made out. How the enemy had succeeded in getting them up to their position it was difficult to ascertain, for the wall was over 20 feet high and only some 3 feet thick. Fire was instantly opened upon the battery by our riflemen. The position, owing to the foliage and the very small part of the wall disturbed, was not easy to locate with the naked eye, but with glasses the gunners could clearly be seen getting their guns into position.

We were not long left in doubt as to the enemy's intentions, for the first missile, a 7-lb round shot, came crashing into the students' quarter, where a group of riflemen were endeavouring to pick off the gunners. The bricks were sent flying in every direction but no harm was done. This was the introduction to several more, all of which took effect on the buildings in the Legation, the Minister's house and upper students' quarters being particularly favoured.

The round shot were of two sizes, one weighing 7 lbs and the other 14 lbs. The bombardment continued with intervals day and night for the next ten days, and over 150 rounds of shot were fired into the Legation and the Hanlin buildings alone. Curiously enough, the only casualty resulting from this fire was an old Chinese woman, whose leg was broken by a round shot, from the effects of which she died. Some people were hurt by falling bricks, displaced by the shot, but no one seriously.

There were, of course, some narrow escapes. The British Nordenfelt, which was temporarily in action on the balcony of the nursery in the Minister's house, was struck by a round shot, which came through the wall and broke the wheel; the seaman who was working the gun escaped uninjured. Another struck a chimney high up, fell down the same and rolled out of the grate on to the floor occupied by three young ladies of the garrison. One crashed through the smok-ing-room of the Minister's house and fell amongst the occupants, all ladies, but without touching any of them. Another, after carrying away part of the coping of one of the bed-rooms in the Minister's house, smashed its way through a thick wall in the escort quarters occupied by the Maritime Customs and fell between two ladies without touching either. And lastly, one entered the big dining-room through the north wall, and passing behind a large picture of the Queen without in any way injuring it, pierced the south wall of the dining-room and fell into the little central garden, where the children were playing at Boxers, barricades, and mimic warfare generally.

Though the enemy's fire from these two batteries —for very shortly a second appeared some 30 yards to the right of the first, also furnished with two smooth bores—was ineffective, the same cannot be said of our return fire, which seemed to annoy the enemy considerably. The invaluable Italian gun was got into position and the second shell exploded in the westernmost battery, completely silencing one gun for the rest of the siege; the others continued to fire at intervals. Our rifle fire was so searching, however, that the gunners were unable to take aim; on the other hand, at that short range they could not help hitting some part of the Legation. The rifle practice, nevertheless, prevented the enemy from concentrat-ing their fire on any one part of our defences and thus making a breach. Very shortly, owing doubtless to their losses at the guns, each embrasure was provided with an iron door, which opened at intervals; the muzzle of the gun was hastily protruded and the gun fired. The opening of these doors was a signal for a volley from our people, who had the range to a nicety. These volleys must have rendered the firing of the gun a somewhat unhealthy occupation.

After the siege was over these batteries were found to consist of very elaborate gun platforms, 20 feet by 16 feet, made of scaffolding strong enough to hold guns of a much heavier calibre than those actually used. They could accommodate from thirty to forty men, and were made of timbers 9 inches in diameter, some 700 to 800 being employed to make each battery. The constructing of the platforms must have taken from a week to ten days, and occupied from thirty to forty workmen a-piece. Ramps 12 feet broad led up to the platforms. A small gallery supported by scaffolding ran along to right and left of the batteries just below the yellow-tiled coping on top of the wall. This gallery was loopholed for musketry. The place where the guns stood was roofed over as a protection from sun and rain. The iron doors mentioned consisted of folding doors on hinges of wrought iron half-an-inch thick, but had been pierced over and over again by our rifle fire, and the left battery had a hole through its door as if made with a punch. This was the work of the Italian gun.

Towards evening the sound of big guns was heard to the west of the city. This was not the bombardment of the Roman Catholic missionary establishment known as the Peitang. The sound came from further off, and was almost due west of the Legation.

6TH JULY

The morning commenced by a severe shell fire against the Fu. The Chinese, emboldened by the failure of our last sortie in this direction, moved one of their Krupp guns up to within a few yards of the wall of the Fu, through which they had made a breach. Colonel Shiba seized the opportunity to make a sortie to capture the gun. Previous to so doing he came to me for orders, and to explain the situation. The gun was located some 10 yards in a lane to the right of the breach above mentioned, and the idea was to dash through the breach and seize the gun and limber. Several Chinese converts provided with ropes for dragging the gun away were to follow the attacking party, which was composed entirely of Japanese marines and volunteers, headed by an ex-officer of the Japanese army serving as a volunteer. A feint attack was to be made from the west by the Italian detachment, reinforced by a corporal and ten British marines.

The Japanese detachment charged through the breach. Unfortunately their leader was almost immediately shot through the throat and fell, but the men pressed on, and actually seized the gun, the Chinese gunners taking to flight. The converts were, however, panic-stricken and refused to advance. The enemy, taking more advantage of their hesitation, rushed back to their loopholes, and a terrific fire was opened upon the attacking party, causing them to retire through the breach with three more of their number *hors de combat*.

The gun and limber were now standing disconsolately in the lane, which formed a *cul de sac*. To venture into the lane was certain death, as every wall and building which commanded it was loopholed, and at every loophole stood one of Tung-fu Hsiang's men with a magazine rifle. On the other hand, any of the enemy who attempted to pass the breach in the wall to get at the gun was shot down by the Japanese. This state of affairs lasted till dark, when the Chinese from their side of the wall threw bricks and stones in front of the breach, gradually filling it up, and during the night they withdrew the gun.

The Russian and French Legations were severely shelled from the Chien Gate, the fire being mainly directed against the American flag, which could be seen from the enemy's battery. At the fourth or fifth shot the flagstaff was struck at the base by a shell, which exploded and shot away a large portion of the roof of the gate-house, bringing down the staff, flag and all. It was rehoisted in a neighbouring tree, the roof of the gate-house being too damaged to allow of it being rehoisted there. The Russian flag was also attracting the fire of this battery, the shooting from which was very true. The flag was therefore removed to another building. It is to be noted that the flags of such Legations as remained unburnt were kept displayed throughout the siege. These were the flags of America, Russia, Great Britain, France, Germany, Japan, and Spain, the Chinese gunners distributing their favours amongst them with absolute impartiality.

A Russian Consular student, whose mind, it appeared, had been somewhat affected by the strain of the siege, suddenly left the French barricade in Legation Street, and, before he could be stopped, advanced alone and unarmed towards the Chinese barricade some 60 yards distant. The enemy allowed him to approach to within 10 yards, and then shot him down. Instantly several Chinese soldiers rushed forward to seize the dead body, but the French sharp-shooters were on the alert, and man after man of the enemy dropped, until eleven had paid the penalty of their temerity with their lives. During the night his body was removed by the Chinese. Since the commencement of the siege this was the third and last European whose dead body fell into Chinese hands. The gallant garrison of the Fu were this day burnt out of some more of the buildings held by them. Since the fighting began they had lost by this means about one quarter of the Fu.

7TH JULY

A quiet morning, but matters became lively as the day advanced. At 9:15 a sharp attack was made against the Fu defences, but repulsed. At 9:30 the French Legation was bombarded by the guns north of the Fu, and also from the Hata Gate. Firing of heavy ordnance was heard to the south and south-west of the city in the direction of the railway terminus. This firing had been distinctly heard throughout the night, and had been reported to me by the officers commanding the French, Austrian, and German detachments, and a notice to this effect was posted on the Bell Tower, and greatly cheered the garrison. The enemy started a fresh barricade near the North Bridge at the end of the road known as "Dusty Lane," but one or two well-placed shells from the Italian gun, which had been brought to the main gate of the Legation, made them desist. The ammunition for this gun was unfortunately getting very low. The cannonading from the Imperial city wall became very brisk; a round shot came through the north corridor of the Minister's house, and fell on the roof of the cellar, which had been converted into a magazine; as this contained some 20,000 rounds of Lee-Metford and Mannlicher ammunition, as well as ninety rounds of shell, common and shrapnel, for the Russian field gun, it was considered advisable to have the cellar further protected by a roofing of sandbags.

There were now only fourteen shells remaining for the Italian quickfirer, so this gun was only used when the case was urgent. The armourer of Her Majesty's ship "Orlando," with considerable ingenuity, devised a new cartridge for the same; taking one of the empty copper cases, most of which had been converted into playthings by the children, but which were now collected, he cast some conical solid shot made from pewter vessels, tea-pots, candlesticks, etc., which had been found in the neighbouring houses; the charge consisted of pebble powder taken from the Russian shells. The difficulty was the percussion cap; this was surmounted by removing the cap of a 45-inch revolver cartridge, which exactly fitted the hole made in the copper case by the removal of the original percussion cap. One of these projectiles was used experimentally in the Italian gun, and answered admirably; the shot being solid pewter, and weighing more than the old shell, the shooting was not so accurate, neither was the effect of the solid shot so good as the explosive shell, but as a makeshift it was excellent. As soon as the shells were finished, these projectiles were taken into use, and continued until the end of the siege; so far as I know, though upwards of seventy were utilized, not one missed fire.

Towards evening much shouting and firing could be heard in the Chinese city; it seemed as if the Boxers and Chinese troops, or different factions of the latter, had fallen out and were settling their differences. Our guards on the wall reported skirmishing between what seemed to be Boxers and Imperial troops, and several of the former were seen to fall.

8TH JULY

At 2 A.M. a very heavy fusillade took place, but lasted only fifteen minutes; it was so severe that the "general attack" bell was rung, and the garrison stood to their arms; the smooth bores on the Imperial city wall joined in the chorus, and the din was deafening.

The morning passed quietly until shortly after 10, when the rattle of musketry burst out all round the north and east of the Fu, accompanied by the fire of the two Krupp guns, which were so close that they made the windows of the British Legation rattle again. At 10:15 the following note was brought to me by a Japanese volunteer:

> Pressed hard; please send a strong reinforcement
> —SHIBA.

Warned by the musketry fire, a reinforcement was in readiness; a non-commissioned officer and six marines, also six volunteers, were at once hurried over. I also wrote to the Russian Legation, and they sent ten sailors; the attack had, however, in the meanwhile, been repulsed, and their services were not required. The French Legation, to whom Colonel Shiba had also applied, had not been able to help, as they were themselves hard pressed, being subjected to a severe shell and rifle fire from the Hata Gate. Captain Thoman, of the Austrian frigate "Zenta," who had come up to Peking as a visitor, and had been unable to return to his ship, was killed on this occasion in the French Legation by a fragment of shell; he was a courteous and gallant officer, and his loss was much felt by those who knew him.

On the previous day one of the gangs of Chinese converts at work under the supervision of Dr Dudgeon discovered at an old foundry within our lines what appeared to be an old piece of iron but proved on closer examination to be a small cannon. The trunnions had been knocked off, and it was one mass of rust and dirt; it was handed over to Mr Mitchell, the master gunner of the American detachment, and after much hard work, scraping and cleaning, it presented quite a creditable appearance. It was at first lashed to a heavy spar; when this was found unsatisfactory, it was mounted on a spare set of wheels belonging to the Italian gun; the shell of the Russian gun, when removed from its projectile, fitted, with some coaxing, the bore of this new gun, which was found on closer examination to be rifled and apparently either made of steel or fitted with a steel lining, and probably dated back to 1860, when the Anglo-French forces were in Peking.

As the gun was found by Chinese converts in charge of a British subject, and was probably of either British or French manufacture; as it fired Russian ammunition, was mounted on an Italian carriage and further was put together and fired by an American, it was with much truth christened the "International" gun, though our marines more often called it the "Dowager-Empress" or "Betsy." The performances of this piece of ordnance were erratic, but owing to the close quarters at which the fighting was carried on, eminently satisfactory.

The first shot was aimed at the corner battery on the Imperial city wall, about 240 yards distant (as there were no sights, the aiming consisted of pointing the gun generally in the direction of the object aimed at). The projectile went screaming over the battery into the Imperial city; the result was received with great cheering by the onlookers in the Legation, who, truth to say, had not much confidence in their new acquisition, and by an astonished silence on the part of the enemy, who were apparently startled to find that after so many days we had at length opened fire with comparatively heavy ordnance. The second shot went woefully short, but the third landed in the battery. This woke the enemy up from their astonishment, and the Mauser bullets began to whistle all round in uncomfortably close proximity; the "International" was therefore temporarily withdrawn, and transported, not without considerable difficulty, over to the Fu, where it was twice fired under Colonel Shiba's orders with telling effect at a barricade some thirty yards distant. The first shot carried away one of the enemy's standards, and the second discharge, which consisted of old nails and bits of scrap iron, was fired into the barricade, and judging from the yells which followed did considerable damage. One drawback to this gun was that immediately the enemy located its whereabouts (which was not at all difficult to do, as the noise and smoke created by it were out of all proportion to its size), they opened a heavy rifle fire on the spot and the gun could not be used for more than three or four shots in succession from the same place. From this evening on, a corporal and five British marines and five volunteers were permanently stationed in the Fu, as affairs were very critical there; the Japanese detachment having been reduced by casualties from one officer and twenty-five men to one officer and seven men, and the Italian detachment had suffered in like manner.

The British marines also supplied a permanent guard of ten men to the American and Russian barricades on the Tartar city wall; this had been the case since the 1st July and lasted till the 17th July; this guard was changed every twenty-four hours. During the afternoon the enemy had been very persistent in their attacks from the Mongol Market and Carriage Park side, they brought up a 1-inch quickfirer and shelled the British Legation; in the space of fifteen minutes three shells exploded inside the roof of the Chinese Secretary's house, the fragments coming through the ceiling in a very unpleasant manner; several of these shells exploded in the trees round the tennis ground, some struck the hospital, which fortunately was well barricaded, and one exploded in front of the Second Secretary's house, then occupied by the Russian Minister's family; the fragments entered a room full of children and buried themselves in the wall and furniture, but happily touched no one. It was impossible to locate this gun as it was skilfully concealed amongst the ruins of the Mongol Market houses and was using smokeless powder; fortunately it never returned to this particular position.

9TH JULY

The "International" gun again changed position. This time it was unlashed from its carriage and hauled up into the Students' Library and fired at a barricade which the enemy had erected in the Carriage Park. Considerable damage was done to the enemy, but nearly every pane of glass was smashed in the library, although the windows were open, and the wall of the mess-room below was cracked. The whole of this day the firing all round was incessant, but nothing of particular interest in the fighting-line occurred. All our positions were maintained; constant work was kept up on the fortifications, repairing the old and making new.

A Christian convert volunteered to go into the city and, if possible, obtain news of what was going on. The American missionaries stated that the man in question was reliable. Towards the evening he returned, having had many narrow escapes. He said that the soldiers that surrounded us were Yung-lu's and Tung-fu Hsiang's men. In the north of the city business was proceeding as usual, the hucksters crying their goods in the streets. He had himself bought some small articles, which he brought back with him. The Emperor and Empress were both at the Palace, only a few hundred yards from us. The "Peking Gazette" was published as usual. The Chinese troops had lost heavily, and were afraid of the foreigners in the Legations. He could hear nothing of any foreign troops coming to our rescue.

10TH JULY

The forenoon was quiet after a night of incessant fusillade. It was evident that the Chinese troops indulged in a siesta between the hours of 11 and 1. During the night they never seemed to sleep; the above hours were, therefore, in future, reserved for demonstrations on our part.

Shortly after 2 a fierce fusillade commenced against the Fu, and the enemy seemed to be concentrating all their efforts on this part of the defence.

Twenty marines under Captain Poole were sent over; also ten Russian marines. One of the Krupp guns suddenly turned its attention from the Fu to the Union Jack over the Legation gateway. Three shells in quick succession struck the gateway, and several exploded on the tennis lawn, just missing the staff.

As the latter was apparently drawing the enemy's fire and thereby endangering the women and children's lives, the question of hauling the flag down, or at any rate, moving it to another position, was mooted to me by the missionaries. Captain Strouts, whom I consulted, was of the opinion that this would only encourage the enemy to further efforts, and would lead to great discontent on the part of the British marine guard. Fortunately the enemy settled the difficulty by turning their attention to other parts of the defence, and never again made a deliberate target of the flag.

11TH JULY

A message carried by one of the Christian refugees was sent out through the water gate. He was received with a volley from a loopholed house opposite, and beat a hasty retreat. The enemy had evidently discovered this means of exit from our lines and were prepared.

During this afternoon Baron von Rahden reported to me that Chinese soldiers had been seen leaving their defences carrying away their bedding, and that heavy firing had been heard south of the Chinese city.

No satisfactory reason for this heavy cannonading to the south and west of the city has ever been given. Rumour said that Prince Ching's troops had fought with Tung-fu Hsiang's and been defeated, but no corroboration of this came to hand.

Mr Nigel Oliphant, who, as already mentioned, had been with the sortie on the Tartar city wall, was brought in from the Fu this afternoon shot through the leg. The day's casualties in the Fu alone amounted to 1 Japanese marine killed and 2 wounded, 2 British marines and 2 volunteers wounded.

The temperature to-day registered 102° in the shade; it had not fallen below 90° for some days. The heat and a perfect plague of flies, together with the stench from dead bodies of men and animals, was very trying, especially for the wounded. The poor living— pony and mule broth—was beginning to tell on the children.

12TH JULY

During the night, which was as noisy as usual, the Chinese built a new barricade in the Imperial Carriage Park enclosure, close to the high west wall of the Hanlin, and also established a sandbag battery on top of it. Behind this they placed a large black silk flag with the Chinese character for "artillery" inscribed thereon. This battery abutted on to our advanced post in the Hanlin. Mr Mitchell, the American gunner, and Sergeant Preston, of the

Marine Guard, in the Hanlin, made a dash for the flag, and jumping up seized it. Instantly a volley of rifle shots went whizzing in all directions: one struck a stone sending the fragments into Sergeant Preston's face; stunned by the blow he let go his hold and fell. Mitchell, however, retained his hold of the flag, and a species of see-saw ensued, with the wall as a fulcrum; several marines and volunteers dashed forward and seized hold of Mitchell. The added weight broke the staff and the flag and part of the staff was triumphantly retained on our side of the wall. This plucky act was the signal for a tremendous outburst of firing from all the enemy's positions which commanded the Hanlin, but our men keeping well under cover no damage was done.

The French garrison the same afternoon made a gallant sortie and captured a large silk flag with scarlet characters on a white ground, setting forth that the flag was presented by the Dowager-Empress to General Ma, commanding the left wing of Yung-lu's army. Dashing forward the French sailors deliberately lassoed the flag and hauled it over to their side of the barricade. A tremendous outburst of rifle-fire was the result, by which, unfortunately, four marines were wounded.

13TH JULY (AND A FRIDAY)

This was the most harassing day for the defence during the whole course of the siege. During the night Tung-fu Hsiang's men had been particularly active in the Hanlin. Shortly after daylight the Fu was heavily shelled by four guns with shrapnel; the defenders could do nothing with such a hail of shot except keep close under cover. The attack became so severe that notwithstanding reinforcements and a most stubborn resistance on the part of the Japanese, Italian, and British, they were compelled to fall back to the last position but one.

Colonel Shiba had originally planned nine lines of defence, one behind the other. The seventh had been held since the 9th instant but had now to be abandoned, as most of its buildings were in flames, and the enemy's Krupp guns were riddling them with common shell and shrapnel shell at a range of 150 yards.

About 4 a tremendous fusillade broke out on all sides. The "general attack" bell sounded, and as many men as could be spared were fallen in ready to reinforce any part of the defences, which were more than usually hard pressed. The firing in the Fu was heavier and more continuous than I have ever heard it before, and accompanied with yells of "Kill, kill," which could be distinctly heard in the Legation; the sound of the firing seemed as if the defenders were being gradually driven back, and I expected every minute to see our people coming out of the Fu gate, crossing the canal, and falling back on to the Legation. I had sent over every man that could be spared, for on all sides we, too, were being attacked.

I wrote to the Russian Legation for reinforcements and very soon ten marines came over at the double. As soon as they had got their breath I sent them over in charge of M. Barbier, a Russian volunteer, who did good service throughout, and who knew the geography of the Fu well. They had hardly disappeared through the gate of the latter when a welcome messenger came from Colonel Shiba to say that he was holding his own and had driven off the enemy, and for the moment required no further men.

I was about to recall the Russians when Herr von Bergen, Second Secretary of the German Legation, came running across the lawn with an urgent written message from the German Chargé d'Affaires, saying that he was very hard pressed and begging for immediate help. The ten Russian marines no longer required at the Fu were at once sent to his aid, and arrived in the nick of time. The enemy, after a smart fusillade, had left their defences and charged into the open with waving banners and loud shouts. They were met by a volley which accounted for six or seven of their number; the rest wavered. The Russians coming up at that moment, the united forces under Lieutenant von Soden charged with fixed bayonets and pursued the enemy capturing one of their standards.

In the meanwhile the French Legation was being vigorously attacked, and shortly after 7 the Chinese exploded two mines underneath the Second Secretary's house and the east side of the Minister's; the explosion completely destroyed these buildings and set fire to those adjacent; two French sailors were killed and buried under the ruins. Captain D'Arcy, the Commandant, was also partially buried and badly cut about the head by falling stones; his wounds were fortunately not serious. The enemy not having properly judged the force of the explosion, suffered severely, and the spy stated that carts next day carried away thirty of their dead from the vicinity of the crater formed by the explosion.

The command of the French detachment for the moment devolved upon Captain Labrousse, an officer of Marine Infantry, a visitor to Peking. When he had satisfied himself that it was impossible to recover the bodies of the buried men, he ordered a retreat to the next line of defence. After the explosion the Chinese, notwithstanding their losses, seemed to be greatly elated at the success of their mining venture and opened a sharp fusillade, but did not leave their defences.

The French and Austrians now occupied a trench which they had prepared, and also the Legation chapel, which was loopholed, and held the enemy at bay. In spite of their severe repulse by the Russian and German detachments, the Chinese attempted another attack along the road leading at the back of the German Legation under the city wall. The Americans were at this moment changing guard at this post; in the half light they detected the attempt, and the double guard opened a withering fire on the advancing enemy, who retired in confusion, leaving twenty dead on the road.

While all this fighting had been going on in the east and north-east, the enemy had also made demonstrations against the Hanlin, but had been kept in check by the fire from the loopholed defences and the upper windows of the students' quarters; just in front of the west corner of the Hanlin defences against the Carriage Park wall there had been a temple; this had been burnt by the enemy on the 23rd June, and only the four walls remained standing. Captain Strouts saw it was important to occupy this enclosure, as the enemy had pushed their attack to within a few yards of it; a hole was made through the wall, and a party under Captain Poole dashed in and occupied the place; a heavy fusillade was opened, but by keeping close to the west wall no one was hit; here two sentry posts were established, so close to the enemy's sandbag entrenchment on the Carriage Park wall, that amenities in the shape of bricks, stones, and water-melon rinds were freely exchanged between the besiegers and besieged, and our sentries could hear the enemy quarrelling over their rice rations and discussing matters generally.

The net result of this day was that the enemy had undoubtedly lost heavily and had been severely handled, and our defences had been pushed forward in the Hanlin, as shown above, but we had lost ground both in the French Legation and in the Fu; our losses amongst the fast diminishing garrison were very serious, amounting to five killed and about double that number wounded.

That evening, together with Colonel Shiba, I inspected the new position in the Fu, to which we had been driven back; the left of the line was pretty strong, consisting of two buildings defended by a high parapet with a species of small fort built against the wall; the ground in front of this was clear, but the enemy had crept up and made a high barricade, its right resting against the wall some 15 yards from the little fort; the parapet was now extended to the right, but unfortunately it was impossible owing to the nature of the ground, to construct it parallel to the enemy's attack, but it fell back considerably, taking in a little artificial mound whereon a redoubt had been constructed. The fort and buildings above mentioned were held by an Italian guard under M. Caetani, Lieutenant Paolini being still incapacitated by his wound. The little hill redoubt was held by Austrians and Italians.

The line then proceeded east some 30 yards, where a building half in ruins was arrived at; this was held by Japanese sailors and volunteers. Looking through the loopholes one could see the enemy's positions amongst the still smoking ruins some 50 yards off; the parapet was carried south-east again till it met a high wall which divided the Su Wang Fu into two portions, the official buildings being on the right and the private dwelling-houses on the left; the defence line followed this till it came to a hole made by the Japanese; here it went due east enclosing two buildings east and west of the big centre gateway to the Prince's official residence.

In front of this entrance was a large courtyard with gates east and west; in this courtyard the Christian converts had originally taken refuge, but had been obliged to abandon it owing to shrapnel and rifle fire; this courtyard formed the right of the line of the Fu defences; it was 260 metres south of the fort held by the Italians, and 220 metres east. The two gates of the courtyard were held by the Japanese marines and British marines and volunteers, the advance sentries being posted by Colonel Shiba and myself at loopholes in the two buildings above mentioned. Looking through these loopholes manned by a British and Japanese sentry side by side, the flames from the burning buildings in front actually touched the muzzles of their rifles. Fortunately, what little wind there was came from the south, increasing in strength as the night advanced; it blew the fire back towards the enemy; but for this the buildings must have caught, the main gate would have followed, and the enemy entering here the whole position would have been taken in reverse. When this fire had burnt itself out our position was strengthened, for it had cleared a space in front of the advanced sentries.

During the night it rained heavily, and the enemy, in consequence, kept up a brisk fusillade; the forenoon was quiet. In the afternoon matters livened up somewhat, and an attack was made on the Russian Legation, the Minister's house being shelled, and his study riddled with shrapnel. The Italian gun was sent over, and assisted in repelling the attack. The "International" went to the French Legation, where, under the able direction of the American gunner it did excellent work, bursting a shell in a Chinese barricade and scattering the enemy.

On this day a Chinese convert, late gatekeeper at the Roman Catholic Cathedral, called the Nan Tang, who had volunteered to take a message to Tien-tsin, came with a letter addressed to me, signed "Prince Ching and others." The messenger bore evidence of having been badly beaten, and he told a sad tale of his experiences. He had been caught attempting to leave the Chinese city, and compelled to give up his letter, which the enemy read. After beating him, they took him to Yung Lu, who ordered that his life should be spared, and handed him this letter. The Roman Catholic missionaries gave the man an indifferent character, so he was kept apart from the rest of the converts, and not allowed to roam about the defences. On the following day he quite willingly took back an answer to Yung Lu.

The enemy having been successful with their mining operations in the French Legation, were evidently bent on trying this means of attack at other points. Sounds of picking were distinctly heard by placing one's ear at the back of our foremost barricade in the Hanlin, close to the Carriage Park wall. Mr Wintour, of the Imperial Maritime Customs, obtained leave and commenced a countermine just at the back of the barricade, and worked in the direction of the sound; three of the Chinese converts, who had proved themselves expert diggers, were told off [assigned to this duty] and put under his orders.

15TH JULY

A quiet night. The Chinese, judging by the sound, were very busy in the early morning in the Carriage Park with pick and shovel, though no signs of what they were at, or exactly where they were, could be detected. One of our marines was brought in danger-ously wounded from the Fu. During the afternoon the Russians made a successful sortie, and pulled down some houses outside their defences, which had been giving cover to the enemy.

At 6:30, Mr Warren, student interpreter, was brought in from the Fu mortally wounded by a splinter of a shell in the face; he died within a few hours without recovering consciousness; he had only been in Peking a few months, and was much liked by his fellow-students.

Heavy firing in the direction of the Peitang, the celebrated Roman Catholic Mission, presided over by Mgr. Favier. We were aware that several thousand refugees, as well as a number of foreign priests and Sisters, were besieged within its walls. When the Legation guards had first come up, a French officer and thirty men, and an Italian officer and eleven men, had been sent to assist in the defence of this important Mission. Though several attempts were made, we never succeeded in establishing communication with this place, which lay only some 4 miles off, but through streets packed with the enemy.

Colonel Shiba reported to me that the men of his detachment, sailors and volunteers, were quite exhausted; they had all been up on duty night and day since the commencement of the siege, and had none of them even changed their clothes since the 20th June, nor had they had more than three or four hours of consecutive sleep during that time; he begged that, if possible, half might be taken off duty for a clear twenty-four hours, and replaced by British marines and volunteers, after which the second half might be relieved in a similar manner. I consulted with Captain Strouts, and it was arranged that, although our people were in the same plight, an effort should be made to carry out Colonel Shiba's wishes. The marines and volunteers responded with alacrity to this call made upon them, for they knew what splendid work the Japanese had done and were doing. It was decided that the Japanese sentries should be relieved by ours at 7 o'clock on the following morning.

16TH JULY

At 7 A.M. Captain Strouts took over the relief party; he was accompanied by Dr Morrison, *The Times* correspondent. After having posted the last sentry, they were returning, and had just left the Italian post, when a shower of bullets came over the barricade, and Captain Strouts fell mortally wounded by a bullet through the groin, which shattered the upper part of the thigh-bone. Dr Morrison was shot almost at the same time by a bullet through the thigh, but which, fortunately, did not strike the bone. Colonel Shiba, who was coming towards them at the time, seeing Captain Strouts and Dr Morrison fall, ran forward to help them; stretchers were procured, and both wounded men were brought into hospital; this was done under heavy fire, a bullet passing through Colonel Shiba's coat.

From the first there was no hope for Captain Strouts, and he died within three hours of his entry into hospital. He was a first-rate officer, cool, calm, and fearless, and his death was a great blow to me and to the entire defence. He was buried at 6 P.M. in the same grave with young Warren, who had been killed the day before. The funeral was attended by all the foreign Representatives, the officers commanding detachments and as many of the garrison as could be spared from their defence duties.

While the mournful procession was proceeding through the Legation grounds to the little cemetery close by the First Secretary's house, the old Chinese messenger who had taken a letter to "Prince Ching and others," bearing a large white flag aloft in one hand, and holding in the other what proved afterwards to be a sufficiently friendly reply to our letter, was marching solemnly along the side of the canal from the North Bridge towards the Legation. The enemy—whether they had in the meantime relented of the friendly tone of the letter he carried, or whether they wished to accelerate their messenger's movements—deftly exploded a shell over his head, fortunately without doing him any harm; the next two shells followed in the same line, exploding in the trees just above the funeral party, but the fragments were carried into the ruins of some neighbouring houses, and did no damage.

The document from "Prince Ching and others," which was an answer to my letter of the previous day, practically initiated a species of armed truce. For the first day or two the enemy were embarrassingly demonstrative in their endeavours to be friendly, and came out unarmed from behind their barricades in considerable numbers, and advanced towards ours. They had repeatedly to be warned back, for we were afraid of treachery; neither did we wish them to see how few were the defenders behind barricades which otherwise looked formidable to them.

As time wore on this friendliness became less and less apparent, and by the end of the month matters had become almost normal, and the attacks and counter-attacks were as brisk and determined as ever.

The precious days of comparative peace which followed the 16th were utilized by us in working with increased energy at our defences. At no time, however, after the 20th of the month was it safe to show for one second outside the defences. The slightest exposure was a signal for a hail of bullets. The old Chinese messenger, besides the official despatch from Prince Ching, brought a cypher telegram for Mr Conger from the State Department at Washington. This, the messenger said, he had received from the Tsung-li Yamên.

The arrival of this telegram created great excitement amongst the besieged, as it was the first news we had had from the outside world since the 18th June. There could be no question of the genuineness of the message, as it was in a cypher possessed only by Mr Conger and the State Department. Mr Conger replied in the same cypher. This message was duly forwarded by the Yamên and duly arrived at Washington, but the public were unwilling to credit it, having apparently quite made up their mind that the Legations had been destroyed, and the besieged massacred.

17TH JULY

At the east barricade in the Fu, the Chinese came from behind their defences in considerable numbers and advanced up to Colonel Shiba's post. Six of them were forthwith made prisoners, the rest beat a hasty retreat. Colonel Shiba reported the matter to me and I ordered the men to be released with a message to their commander to the effect that if more than two left their barricades together they would be fired on.

The same afternoon I was on the Tartar city wall, inspecting the defences, together with Mr Squiers, whom I had appointed Chief of the Staff. The Colonel commanding Tung-fu Hsiang's troops in the opposing barricade, some sixty yards off, had shouted a message across for permission to bury his dead which were lying at the foot of our barricade, the result of the sortie of the 3rd instant. This permission, as may be imagined, was readily granted.

The Chinese barricade was swarming with men, at least 250 being crowded on it and the adjacent walls; their arms were all out of sight. They were dressed in a variety of uniforms, scarlet and black of Tung-fu Hsiang's men predominating. Six of the Chinese soldiery descended with spades and large pieces of matting, on which they proceeded to carry away the rotting corpses. Through Mr Splingard, our interpreter, I requested the Colonel to come and have a talk with me. After some demur he consented. I offered him a cigar, which he gladly accepted, and we sat on the outside of our barricade and chatted until our cigars were finished. He told me that he belonged to the Kansu troops, but was at present under the immediate orders of Yung Lu, who was desirous of stopping the fighting. I remarked that the fighting was none of our doing, but we were quite prepared to defend ourselves whenever attacked. I said that, to prevent misunderstandings, it would be better if not more than two men left their barricades at a time. If more than that number did so I should be compelled to open fire. He said he thought it would be a good thing if some such understanding were arrived at, and suggested my writing a letter to Yung Lu to this effect. He assured me that any letter handed to him for Yung Lu would most certainly reach its destination. On my return, whilst standing on the top of our barricade, I could see the enemy's positions stretching away to the north until they disappeared in the direction of the Carriage Park.

There were barricades in the streets below the wall. A large temple was loopholed and put into a state of defence and full of men. More men were amongst the ruins west of the Russian Legation, and a species of mound which commanded this Legation and the Mongol Market was gay with the uniforms of hundreds of Imperial infantry. Following the line west of the Mongol Market the tops of the houses carried nests of these brightcoated soldiery. Altogether from my position I saw some 1,500 to 2,000 men, and many more must have been hidden behind the walls and ruined houses. From where I stood I noticed that the men in the opposing barricade could overlook certain portions of our position on the wall, and would probably remark on the very small garrison we were able to maintain. I therefore requested the American and Russian Commandants to send up as many of their reserve men as could be spared, with orders to show themselves as much as possible on the barricades. This order was promptly and quietly carried out, and very shortly our position was occupied by a goodly number of Russian and American sailors, as well as by some twenty of our marines.

On my return to the Legation I wrote a despatch to Yung Lu, and stated that in view of the negotiations which had commenced with the Tsung-li Yamên the defenders of the Legation would not fire unless they were fired at, but to prevent misunderstandings it would be better if not more than two soldiers left their barricades, and these must be unarmed. Any armed soldier leaving his barricade would at once be fired at. I also added that if the enemy were seen making new barricades in advance of those already existing, fire would be opened on the working parties, even if they were unarmed. This letter was delivered into the hands of my friend the Colonel, who promised to deliver it to Yung Lu.

The Commanders of all portions of the defence reported that the enemy had ceased firing, and showed a friendly disposition and a desire to enter into conversation with the besieged. This was much less the case in the north and west, where they were decidedly treacherous and unfriendly, though they had evidently received the same orders as their comrades. From information picked up by the Japanese at their barricade it was evident that the cause of this sudden change in the demeanour of our assailants was due to the news which the high authorities, whoever they may have been at that time, had received of the capture of the native city of Tientsin by the allies, and the rout of the Chinese army. By some friendly soldiers we were warned against mines which were especially to be directed against the British Legation. In addition to the countermine begun by Mr Wintour on the 14th, and which by now had been sunk to a depth of some 9 feet, and then for a short distance carried under the Carriage Park wall, a system of countermines had been organized in the north and west of the Legation, and carried out most efficiently under Mr Gamewell's direction. They consisted of trenches some 11 or 12 feet deep close up against our advanced lines, and it would have been impossible for the enemy to pass these trenches without being immediately detected.

18TH TO 19TH JULY

On the 18th July a messenger who had been sent out by Colonel Shiba returned from Tien-tsin with a letter from the Japanese head-quarters staff at that place. It contained the news that the native city had been taken by the allies, and that a relief force was being organized consisting of 24,000 Japanese, 4,000 Russians, 2,000 British, 1,500 Americans, and 1,500 French, and would leave on or about the 20th July and advance on Peking. This notice was posted on the Bell

Tower. It was the first news we had had from Tien-tsin, and was joyfully welcomed by the besieged, though many were disappointed that the force was not already well on its way. In fact the message was far less hopeful. It mentioned the heavy losses sustained by the allies, and also spoke of the absolute absence of transport. To keep up the spirits of the besieged, however, the message as posted was made as cheerful as possible.

As an instance of the curious state of affairs which existed at this time between the besiegers and besieged, especially on the east side where the Japanese and French were in contact with the enemy, a young Frenchman, by name Pelliot, wandered over to the opposing barricade and entered into conversation with the Chinese soldiery; without thinking he stepped inside their barricade and was instantly made prisoner; he was not roughly treated but taken to a Yamên at some distance where he was brought before some high Mandarins who courteously asked him several questions regarding our strength, losses, etc., all of which he answered in an evasive manner; eventually he was conducted under an escort of Yung Lu's men through streets full of Boxers and soldiery, back to the barricade, and set at liberty.

The Japanese started a small market for eggs which the Chinese soldiers brought over hidden in their capacious sleeves and sold to our people; the eggs were mostly distributed by the Food Supply Committee to the hospital, and amongst the women and children. The weather was very hot and the latter began to feel the want of proper food; six of the younger ones were to die in the Legation.

20TH TO 27TH JULY

On the 20th it was reported to me that the Chinese were heard mining in close proximity to the Hanlin. I went down Mr Wintour's counter-mine and heard them distinctly at work; they seemed quite close but somewhat above my level; a pick was handed down and at the first few blows the enemy stopped working. From that time a strict watch was kept at this countermine, but the enemy had either abandoned their mine or had changed direction, for the sounds gradually died away and then stopped altogether.

Later the mine was thoroughly examined by the Royal Engineers; it was found to commence in one of the large buildings in the Carriage Park enclosure and to proceed straight for our barricade in the Hanlin. It arrived within a few feet of Mr Wintour's countermine and then suddenly changed direction to the south and followed parallel to the dividing wall for some 40 feet, till it arrived opposite the centre of the building, forming the students' library and mess-room when, instead of turning east under this building, it turned west, described a curve and ended at a point some 30 yards due south of where it started. There is no doubt that Mr Wintour's countermine checked the enemy's advance underground and headed them south, but why, when they got to a convenient striking point, they went away from their objective, it is impossible to say.

During this spell of comparative quiet the enemy were very busy working at their barricades, and besides the one I have mentioned, mines were started by them on the top of the Tartar city wall endeavouring to get under the Russo-American barricade, also in Legation Street working towards the Russian barricade; similar mines were commenced against the French and Japanese defences on the east; we, in the meanwhile, were equally busy working at our defences and countermines.

Later, a letter was found addressed to the General Commanding at the Hata Men, on the subject of mines. The writer had been a teacher at the British

Legation in the employ of Her Majesty's Government for four years and was well known to the student interpreters; together with all the other teachers he disappeared about the middle of June. The letter was dated the beginning of July and pointed out that the General's methods of attacking the Legation were faulty and were bound to lead to considerable loss in the future as they had done in the past. The proper method of attack, the writer said, was by mining; to assist the General in his attack he enclosed a correct plan of the British Legation, with which he was well acquainted, and marked on the plan the most suitable place for the mine to be driven. Eager inquiries have been made since the siege was raised for the writer of the letter but as yet he has not been found.

On the 18th July one of Yung Lu's men advanced with a flag of truce along the city wall, and came down to the German defences with a letter for me from Yung Lu, accepting the arrangement suggested with regard to terms of a truce. This man was very intelligent and friendly; he had been specially selected to come, as he had had to deal with foreigners, having been a police-man on the Peking–Tien-tsin Railway. He was recognized by one or two Europeans in the Legation. The same afternoon another soldier came in with his ear partially severed; he had been in the employ of Sir Robert Hart, and was bugler to the regiment at the Hata Gate. He came in, he said, to have his ear seen to, as he knew that foreign surgeons were good and humane men. His officer had wounded him with a blow of his sword for not being sufficiently proficient on his bugle. He informed us, further, that the men were very discontented, and were sick of fighting the foreigners. The same story was told by three soldiers who strolled along the wall from the direction of the Hata Gate to the American barricade.

It was very evident throughout the siege that the enemy on the east were much more friendly, and had not the same stomach for fighting as our friends in the north and west; from this direction not a single man ever came in, neither did any of our messengers ever succeed in getting out. My conversation with the Colonel on the city wall was the only instance of a friendly act on that side.

Even when the truce was at its height, from the 17th to the 20th, it was unsafe to show oneself for an instant at the barricades in the Hanlin. On the 19th some of the enemy held out a water melon at the end of a pole on one of the Hanlin barricades; a volunteer of ours advanced to take it, and was instantly fired at, the bullet passing within an inch of his head.

On the 20th and subsequent days several of our people, mostly Chinese converts, were hit whilst working at the defences; this was, of course, in accordance with the terms of truce, and we returned the compliment.

On the 24th the supply of eggs began to dwindle down, and the men who brought them reported to the Japanese that their officers had threatened to execute anybody found bringing in anything to the besieged. On the 23rd two men were beheaded for this reason within sight of the Japanese.

28TH JULY

On the 28th July the boy messenger, who had been sent out on the 4th July, returned from Tien-tsin. His arrival caused great excitement; he brought, sowed in the collar of his coat, the British Consul's letter in answer to mine. The news ran like wildfire through the Legation, and eager crowds surrounded the Bell Tower, waiting to hear what was posted on the notice board. This was the message:

Yours of the 4th July. 24,000 troops have now landed, and 19,000 here. General Gaselee expected Taku to-morrow. Russians hold Pei Tsan. Tien-tsin city under foreign Government, and Boxer power has exploded. Plenty of troops are on the way if you can hold out with food. Almost all ladies have left Tien-tsin.

This letter caused great disappointment amongst the garrison, as the general opinion was that ample time had elapsed between the 20th June and the 21st July to organize and start a relief expedition.

In justice to Mr Carles, who has been blamed for not sending more information, it is right to state that, had he written the true state of affairs which then existed in Tien-tsin, the effect on the beleaguered garrison would have been crushing; he consequently made the note as cheerful as he could under the circumstances. Had not the arrival of the messenger been witnessed by numbers of people, it is more than probable no notice of the contents of the letter would have been posted on the Bell Tower.

During the early days of the armistice from their barricades on the east of the Fu, the Chinese adopted a novel way of communicating with the Japanese defenders. One day a large dog trotted into the Japanese barricade with a note tied round its neck. This was from the Chinese General commanding in that quarter, pointing out the futility of further defence, and recommending unconditional surrender. A reply, declining the suggestion in somewhat forcible terms, was tied on the dog's neck, with which it trotted back.

This was repeated several times, the advisability of surrender being urged with greater insistence each time. The answers varied only in the strength of their language. Letters demanding and suggesting surrender were also tied to arrows and shot into the Japanese lines. A remarkable instance which took place at this time of filial obedience and good faith on the part of a Chinese soldier, was recounted to me by Colonel Shiba.

Amongst the men who brought eggs for sale was one who belonged to Yung Lu's force, who was distinguished from his fellows by the hard bargains which he drove for his wares. Noticing this, Colonel Shiba thought the man might be induced for a price to carry a letter to Tien-tsin and bring back an answer. He was accordingly approached on the subject, and after considerable discussion about the amount, he agreed to go for the sum of 250 dollars, the money to be paid over on his return with the answer. The man left on the 22nd and returned on the 1st August, bringing with him a reply from the Chief of staff of the Japanese division. It ran as follows:

> Your letter of 22nd received. Departure of troops from Tien-tsin delayed by difficulties of transport, but advance will be made in two or three days. Will write again as soon as estimated date of arrival at Peking is fixed.

The letter was dated the 26th July. The bearer refused to accept the 250 dollars, and no amount of persua-

sion could induce him to do so. Thinking that perhaps he was unwilling to be discovered in possession
of so large a sum, he was offered a letter to the Consul
at Tien-tsin in the form of a promissory note, but he
declined everything. On being asked why he refused
now, when he had been previously so keen to acquire
the money, he told Colonel Shiba that on arrival at
Tien-tsin, after delivery of the letter and receiving the
answer, he went to his own home; his mother did all
she could to prevent his returning to Peking, but he
said he had promised the foreign officer to return, and
return he must. "Then," said she, "you must accept no
money, for what you are doing is for the good of your
country." He, therefore, in obedience to his mother's
wishes, steadfastly refused any money whatever. He
offered to take a letter back to Tien-tsin if it was written at once, but he could not, he said, bring back an
answer. Seeing that it was impossible to shake the
man's resolution, Colonel Shiba wrote another letter
which the messenger duly delivered at the Consulate
at Tien-tsin, but again refused all offers of money.

29TH JULY TO 1ST AUGUST

On the afternoon of the 29th July the Chinese began to throw out heaps of bricks and stones at the corner of some ruined houses at the east end of the north bridge. This bridge was commanded by the north stable picket, and by a caponier which had been constructed in front of the main gate of the Legation, called by the marines "Fort Halliday." The road across it is one of the main arteries of the city from east to west, and to avoid the bridge the Chinese had to make a considerable detour through the Imperial city. It had always been a source of surprise to us that no barricade had been constructed across the bridge, because in addition to allowing passage across, the fire from it, the barricade, would command the whole length of the canal with the roads on either side, and would sweep the south bridge, which was one of our means of communication (the only one for carts), between the east and west defences. During the night-time the bridge was undoubtedly used by the enemy; but in the daylight the fire of our pickets was so deadly, that after losing several men, they gave up all attempts at crossing it.

It soon became evident that the heap of bricks and stones was the commencement of the long-expected barricade; immediately a lively fusillade was opened on the inoffensive-looking heap, and bricks and stones were sent flying, but so soon as they were shot away others appeared in their place. Very shortly wooden cases, evidently filled with bricks and stones, were pushed forward from behind the heap and the barricade stealthily crept forward.

The enemy's sharpshooters in the ruins on the other side of the canal were in the meanwhile very busy, and some very pretty shooting took place. They had the most modern rifle with smokeless powder, and the men in the north stable picket had some very narrow escapes, bullets pattering round their loop-holes and in some instances coming through.

The "International" gun was at that time doing good service in the French Legation so could not be used, but the Italian 1-pr. with its solid pewter bullet was hauled up on to a sandbag battery on the roof of the cow-house which formed part of the north stable picket, and opened fire. The enemy were not slow to return the compliment, and the Mauser bullets soon began to knock the sandbags about, at the close range of 60 yards, cutting them into shreds.

The Italian gunner behaved with great coolness. Unfortunately, as he was laying the gun for the third round his hand was smashed by a Mauser bullet, and he was taken to hospital. The sergeant commanding the marine detachment went up and fired the round, but the enemy's fire now became so hot, pieces of silk damask and sand being scattered in every direction by the hail of bullets. It was found impossible to continue the gun in action; it was also impossible to remove it. This was eventually done under cover of darkness.

On the following morning it was found that the enemy had succeeded in building a barricade 6 foot high the whole length of the north bridge, a distance of 30 to 40 yards.

In the correspondence which was at this time proceeding between the Diplomatic Body and the Chinese Government as represented by "Prince Ching and others," expostulations had been made respecting the strengthening of our defences. Attention was, therefore, drawn to the building of this formidable barricade by the Chinese Imperial troops. The reply received was that "we must not be alarmed as the troops of Tung-fu Hsiang were only engaged in mending the road!"

Fire was immediately opened from this barricade, and the road along the canal became very dangerous. To obviate this a large traverse was run across the road at the smaller gate of the Legation and a barricade constructed across the south bridge.

2ND TO 6TH AUGUST

On the 2nd August the fortifications having been thoroughly strengthened on the north and east, it was determined to improve our western defences. Consequently, a small party of British marines and volunteers of various nationalities, mostly belonging to the Imperial Maritime Customs, under M. von Strauch, an ex-officer of the German army, were directed to cut a hole through the west wall of the stable quarters and occupy some buildings forming

the east side of the Mongol Market. The hour chosen was that of the Chinese siesta, shortly before
noon. The houses were successfully occupied without the enemy becoming aware of our intentions.
They were found to be in a good state of preservation, and a party of Christian converts under Mr
Gamewell's orders were at once set to work to
loophole the walls and make barricades where necessary. Three Chinese soldiers were found dead in
the houses, where they had evidently dragged
themselves to die.

In a few days this position, which was one of
considerable importance, was greatly strengthened.
Thus on the north and west the British Legation
defences had been pushed forward in the direction
of the enemy. The latter very soon discovered this
new occupation, and the whole of the Mongol
Market barricades blazed out on our working parties. These, however, kept well under cover, and only
a few casualties took place.

For the remaining few days of the siege this position was the scene of constant attack. The enemy,
whose barricades by the Carriage Park wall were
within stone-throwing distance, kept up a constant
fire, also hurling bricks and stones over the ruined
walls. One of our marines was badly cut on the head
by one of these missiles.

On this day a messenger arrived from Tien-tsin
bearing many letters. The following were posted on
the Bell Tower:

From the American consul, Tien-tsin, to American Minister, dated the 28th July.

Had lost all hope of seeing you again. Prospect now brighter. We had thirty days shelling here, nine days siege, thought that bad enough. Scarcely a house escaped damage. Excitement at home is intense; of course, our prayers and hopes are for your safety and speedy rescue. Advance of troops to-morrow probable.

Another from Lieutenant-Colonel Mallory, United States' Army, dated the 30th July:

A relief column of 10,000 is on the point of starting for Peking; more to follow. God grant they may be in time.

The one which contained the most news was written by Mr Lowry, of the American Legation, who was in Tien-tsin when the railway was cut. The letter was to his wife, one of the besieged. It was as follows:

The bearer arrived last Friday with news from Peking. The 9th, 14th United States' Regiments already at Tien-tsin. 6th Cavalry at Taku on its way up. An advance guard of several regiments has already started. There was fighting this morning at Pei Tsang. Everything is quiet here now. Word came to-day Boxers killing Christians at Tsun Hua and many other places. Tien-tsin full of foreign troops and more coming all the time. Railway open between here and Tangku. Many ladies and children went back to United States on transport "Logan." All property at Pei-tai Hoa destroyed.

This letter was dated the 30th July.

This news greatly cheered the spirits of the garrison.

7TH TO 9TH AUGUST

On the 7th August "Prince Ching and others" sent condolences on the death of the Duke of Saxe-Coburg and Gotha and the firing was heavier than usual. The enemy seemed now to be concentrating their attention on the British Legation, the fire from the Mongol Market being particularly severe; the bullets were also coming lower. Mr Gamewell reported that our fortifications in this quarter were being damaged by rifle fire to an extent which had not before occurred. We ascertained afterwards through spies that a new division of troops had come from Shansi under a Brigadier-General, who had sworn to take the Legation in five days. This division was stationed in the Mongol Market.

Orders were posted on the Bell Tower that women and children were not to walk about the grounds while firing was going on, several very narrow escapes having taken place. To meet the attacks from the west the Nordenfelt was mounted on a platform on the top of the wall at the back of the Chinese Secretary's house and did excellent work. A platform was also made in our new defences in the Mongol Market for the "International" gun, which was still in charge of the indefatigable American gunner, Mitchell.

On the 9th August the Fu, which had enjoyed a spell of comparative quiet, was again attacked, and fresh flags were planted behind the enemy's barricades. The attack was evidently now closing in. We had, however, worked so hard on the defences that our casualties were very few.

10TH AUGUST

At 3 in the afternoon a tremendous fusillade took place against the Fu and all our defences, Hanlin, Carriage Park, and Mongol Market. The big gun fire had entirely ceased since the commencement of the armistice, but the rifle fire was very heavy, and cut our fortifications about considerably.

On this day a messenger, who had been sent out on the 6th to the advancing forces, returned with the following letter from General Gaselee, dated the 8th August, Tsai Tsung:

> Strong force of allies advancing. Twice defeated enemy. Keep up your spirits.

Colonel Shiba also received a letter from General Fukushima, dated Camp at Chong Chiang, 2 P.M., north of Nan Tsai Tsung, the 8th August:

> Japanese and American troops defeated enemy on 5th instant near Pei-tsang and occupied Yang-tsun. The allied force, consisting of Americans, British, and Russians, left Yang-tsun this morning, and while marching north I received your letter at 8 P.M. at a village called Nan Tsai Tsung. It is very gratifying to know that the foreign community at Peking are holding on, and believe me it is the earnest and unanimous desire of the Lieutenant-General and all of us to arrive at Peking as soon as possible, and relieve you from your perilous position. Unless some unforeseen event takes place the allied force will be at Ho Si Wu on the 9th, Matou, 10th, Chang Chin-wan, 11th, Tung Chou, 12th, and arrive Peking 13th or 14th.

On the 6th Mr Squiers, my Chief of the staff, had drawn up a plan of the city, showing the sluice gate through the Tartar city wall, and our position on the wall, which was marked by three flags, a Russian on the western extremity, a British flag in the centre, and an American on the east. Directions were given in this letter in English and American cypher as to the best means of entrance. The letter was addressed to the American and English Generals, and was duly delivered to them on the 8th instant.

12TH AUGUST

From the various quarters of the defence reports came in that the enemy were very active, and it became evident that the relief force was nearing. From the Russo-American position on the Tartar city wall numerous bodies of troops were reported leaving the Cheng Meng. From the north stable picket bodies of cavalry were seen to advance up to the bridge, dismount, and lead their horses across under cover of the barricade; their movements were considerably accelerated by our riflemen from that post and the Main Gate caponier; the Krupp gun by the Hata Gate, which had been silent for several days, again opened fire. Nickel-plated bullets, fired at a range of 20 yards, pierced our defences in the Mongol Market and elsewhere. In their eagerness to press forward, the enemy overthrew one of their own barricades. Instantly our sharpshooters opened a deadly fire, and the Nordenfelt was brought to bear. Before they could escape this hail of bullets twenty-seven, including their leader, fell in a riddled heap. The next day "Prince Ching and others" wrote an indignant protest, saying that the "converts" had again opened fire on the Imperial troops, killing an officer and twenty-six men. We subsequently heard that the officer was none other than the General of Division whose rash oath has been recorded.

When the evening closed in the enemy had made no advance in any direction and had lost severely. Our casualties were few, but they included Captain Labrousse, of the French Staff, an officer who had done excellent service both in the French Legation and on the Tartar city wall; in this capacity he came particularly under my notice, his reports being very lucid and of great service to the defence. In him the French army lost a smart and capable officer.

13TH AUGUST

The morning of the 13th commenced with sharp firing in every direction, which lasted with scarcely an interval throughout the day. Towards evening it was reported to me that the enemy were at work in the battery on the Imperial city wall. I immediately, proceeded to the north stable picket, and, in the failing light, through glasses, saw that work of some kind was being carried on. The sergeant of the picket reported that previous to my arrival he had seen what he thought was a modern piece of artillery owing to the light catching on brass mountings. As the enemy had not fired from this battery since the 16th July, I thought that it would be advisable to let sleeping dogs lie and not to draw the fire unnecessarily, especially as the relief force was so close; but, to be on the safe side, before the light died away altogether the Austrian Maxim was brought into the north stable and careful aim taken at the battery. The American gunner in charge of the automatic Colt, in the Main Gate caponier, was instructed also to lay his gun on the embrasure. Both had orders that immediately fire was opened from it the two machine-guns were to return the fire. The ranges were 200 and 350 yards.

Shortly before 8 a tremendous rifle fire opened all round, and instantly the above-mentioned battery joined in. The sergeant had been right in his surmise, for, instead of our old friend the smooth bore, it was a 2-inch quick-firing Krupp which opened on us with segment and common shell. Hardly had the crash of the first exploding shell taken place when the Austrian Maxim and the American Colt rattled out their reply. At the seventh round this gun was silenced, but not before it had done considerable damage; three shots struck Fort Halliday, stunning the inmates, though hurting nobody; one carried away a tall chimney in the Minister's house, another struck a brick pillar in the upstairs balcony of the north-east corner of said house (a post commonly known as Rosamond's Bower), completely demolishing the pillar and part of the balcony, and one pierced the roof and exploded in my dressing-room, creating very considerable havoc; fortunately, not a single casualty resulted from all this cannonade.

14TH AUGUST

Four times between sunset and sunrise the "general attack" bell was sounded, when all reserves turned out and stood ready for emergencies. The enemy seemed particularly active in the Mongol Market; reinforcements were urgently requested from this quarter, and were promptly sent. The Chinese officers were heard inciting the men to charge, laying stress on the fact that they far outnumbered us and the distance was very short. The firing ceased, and an ominous silence followed, as if they were in reality gathering for the attack. It was then that our Commandant sent for reinforcements; before they arrived the enemy had evidently thought better of their intention to attack with the bayonet, and had recommenced firing and throwing bricks. The din of rifle fire, the rattle of bullets on the roofs, and the scream and crash of large ordnance was deafening.

At about 2 A.M. there was a pause, when very distinctly the delighted garrison heard the boom of heavier guns away to the east and the sound of many Maxims evidently outside the city walls. The scene in the Legation was indescribable. Those who, tired out, had fallen asleep were wakened by these unwonted sounds, and there was much cheering and shaking of hands. The enemy, too, had heard it. For a moment there was silence; then the rifle fire broke out more angry and deafening than before, instantly responded to by the rattle of our sharpshooters and the grunt of the five-barrelled Nordenfelt, which, under the able management of the "Orlando's" armourer and Sergeant Murphy of the marines, refused to jam, but hailed volleys of bullets into the Mongol Market barricades.

The "International" was also particularly active, and fired at point blank range into the said barricade until the gallant gunner Mitchell had his arm badly broken by a Mauser bullet, and was taken to hospital. After the siege had ended, the little garrison of the Mongol Market defences found that the "International" was loaded, but owing to the accident to the gunner had not been fired. As it was impossible to draw the charge, the muzzle was elevated, and the last shot fired from this unique gun descended amongst the yellow-tiled pavilions of the Pink or Forbidden City.

With daylight the firing died down, and there was a period of calm. A sharp look-out was kept from all the posts, especially the Tartar city wall, for any possible appearance of the relieving force. Mr Squiers, my energetic Chief of the staff, reported from the American Legation shortly after daybreak: "On the wall there has been no sign of the approach of our troops beyond the firing of the machine-guns. The direction of the firing seemed to be the Chinese wall just to the right of the part where it joins the Tartar city wall. There is no commotion in the Chinese city or at either of the gates. Your flag-staff was shot away during the night, the flag falling over the wall. Fortunately it was secured, and pulled back before the Chinese had a chance to capture it. If you will send a carpenter I will attend to repairs." The armourer and signalman of the "Orlando" were sent, the staff was mended, and the flag rehoisted.

At 6 A.M. Mr Squiers again reported: "The Chinese have three guns mounted at the Hata Men, which they have been firing in an easterly direction. All the musketry fire seemed to be on the wall between the Hata Men and the tower at the corner. No excitement in the Chinese city. The Chien Men is still open, but few passing in or out." Again, at 7 A.M.: "Heavy firing at the Chi-hua Men; also further

machine-gun fire beyond the Hata Men. No movement in the Chinese city." This was the Japanese,
Russian, and American attack developing along the
east side of the Tartar city. As can be seen, Mr Squiers
is careful to report any movement in the Chinese city,
for in accordance with the plan sent out it was in this
direction the relief was expected. At 9.15 he reports:
"For the past half-hour Chinese soldiers have been
pouring out of the Chien Men, going in the direction
of the south gate; cavalry, infantry, and two pieces of
artillery. In the direction of the Hata Men there is
heavy cannon fire, and a large shell has just exploded
in the roof of the tower in the south-east angle of the
Tartar city."

At 11 the report came: "Large numbers of
Chinese soldiers are passing through the Chien Men
into the Imperial city." The defending troops were
evidently being withdrawn from the Chinese city to
meet the Japanese attack on the east gate of the
Tartar city.

Shortly before 3 P.M. a breathless messenger from
the Tartar city wall arrived to say that foreign troops
were under the city wall opposite the water gate. I
immediately followed him, and arrived in time to
receive General Gaselee and his staff as they came
through the said gate and stood on the canal road.
From there I led them through the Russian Legation
to the British, where they were welcomed by the rest
of the besieged garrison. The regiment which first
entered the Legation quarter was the 7th Rajpoots
under Major Vaughan. With them was Major Scott, of

the 3rd Sikhs, attached to the 1st Sikhs, with a few men of this regiment. This officer with several men ran along the canal road from the south bridge to the gateway opposite the First Secretary's house, and were the first to enter the British Legation. This portion of the canal road was under the enemy's fire from the north bridge barricade, and three casualties occurred here later in the afternoon.

On arriving in the Legation, which was still being hotly attacked by the enemy form the Hanlin and Mongol Market, a small detachment of the 7th was sent into the Main Gate caponier to assist in repelling the attack. A man of this regiment was almost immediately seriously wounded; one of the ladies of the garrison was also wounded on the lawn. In the meanwhile, Mr Squiers with a small party of Russian and American marines, under Captain Vroubleffsky and Captain Perry Smith, had proceeded along Legation Street to the Chien Gate, which they opened, allowing the 1st Sikhs, under Colonel Pollock and the Hong Kong artillery to enter, the Chinese making a stand here and charging up to the Maxims of the artillery. The American troops under General Chaffey, and Russians under General Linievitch had, with considerable loss, forced the north-east gate of the Chinese city, and proceeding underneath the wall, had entered, some by the water gate and some by the Chien Gate. Two guns of Major Johnson's Battery Royal Artillery had also been got through the water gate and up an improvised ramp on to the canal road. One of these guns was brought on to the south bridge, and effectively shelled the north bridge barricade, and the battery on the Imperial city wall.

The besieged lost no time in taking the offensive. As has been seen, the American and Russian Legations were instrumental in opening the Chien Gate; Lieutenant von Soden with a detachment of his men attacked the enemy and drove them to the Hata Gate, capturing their guns and banners; the Italian and Japanese detachment in the Fu drove the enemy from their positions and reoccupied the entire Fu.

A detachment of British marines and volunteers under Captain Poole cut a hole through the Carriage Park wall and occupied the whole of this enclosure, killing three of the enemy.

Two days later a detachment of French, Russian, and English troops relieved our gallant fellow prisoners in the Pei-tang, whose sufferings had been worse than ours, and the siege of Peking came to an end.

END OF THE SIEGE

During the siege the following number of cases passed through the International Hospital: 126 wounded, all severely, of whom 17 died; 40 cases of sickness, mostly anteric and dysentry, of whom 2 died. Of the 166 cases treated 142 were soldiers or sailors, the rest civilians; 165 were men; 1 woman was wounded. Of the above cases 21 were Germans; Americans, 17; English 55; French, 17; Dutch, 1; Japanese, 14; Italians, 17; Austrians, 6; and Russians, 18.

The slightly wounded are not mentioned in this Return; many of these were treated on the spot by the excellent French and Japanese military surgeons, who remained with their detachments in the French Legation and Fu.

The latter post has frequently been mentioned as the scene of severe fighting. The following Return of the numbers killed and wounded therein will be of interest:

	Killed	Wounded
English	2	11
French	1	2
Russians	0	2
Austrians	1	1
Italians	7	11
Japanese	9	21
Chinese	18	85
Total	38	133

The Chinese were mostly employed working in the defences, though Colonel Shiba had organized a force of some twenty Chinese armed with swords and spears who were very useful in keeping watch.

A Return of the officers killed and wounded of the various marine detachments will be of interest:

	Officers arrived	Killed	Wounded
British	3	1	2
Italians	2	0	2
Russians	2	0	0
Japanese	2	1	1
German	1	0	0
French	3	2	1
Austrians	4	1	2
Americans	2	0	1
Total	19	5	9

The total number of foreigners killed during the siege from the 20th June to the 14th July inclusive, was sixty-six.

From the 20th June to the 13th July the garrisons of the Su Wang Fu and the French Legation were driven back step by step, disputing every inch of the ground, yielding only to superior numbers and having to cope with shell fire, incendiarism, and in the case of the French Legation, subterranean mines, until, after twenty-three days' fighting, three quarters of each of these two positions was in the hands of the enemy. Had the latter pressed on after the 13th July with the same persistence they showed up to that date, and also having an attenuated and worn-out garrison to deal with, they would have captured both positions by the 20th July at latest. Fortunately, on the 14th instant, Tien-tsin was taken by the allies; this produced a marked effect on the besiegers, and the besieged received nearly twenty days' respite, which enabled them to materially strengthen their defences and recuperate generally, so that the final attacks of the enemy were repulsed with ease.

Sir C. MacDonald to the Marquess of Lansdowne
(received February 2, 1901)

My Lord,   *Tôkiô, December* 26, 1900

In my Report dated the 20th September last, I had the honour to recommend certain officers and civilians who performed exceptionally good service during the siege of Peking.

To the names then mentioned, it gives me great pleasure to add the names of the following gentlemen volunteers, members of the Imperial Maritime Customs, whose services have been specially brought to my notice by Captain Poole, who was in charge of volunteers.

CLAUDE M. MACDONALD

Enclosure

List of Members of the Imperial Maritime Customs recommended by Sir C. MacDonald

Mr Macoun was for some time in charge of the Customs contingent of volunteers, arranged their roster, and was himself unceasingly on duty in either the dangerous Prince Su's Park or West Hanlin. He was an indefatigable worker. He was wounded in the thigh by a bullet in Prince Su's Park on the 12th July, and, though lame from the effects, cheerfully resumed his duties after a week's rest. I understand that he is not even now fully recovered.

Mr de Courcy was also conspicuous by his hard work, and cheerfully resumed his dangerous duty in the park and elsewhere before his health really rendered it advisable for him to do so. After the siege his health completely broke down, and he died at Tientsin on the 29th September. He was also slightly wounded in the Legation compound.

Mr Smythe, too ill at the commencement for work, took his duty at the very earliest opportunity, and was always only too eager to supplement his own watches by relieving those who were worn out by the extreme length of the watches towards the end of the siege. His health suffered severely under the strain of his self-denying good nature, resulting in an attack of typhoid after the relief.

Mr Bethell's extreme youth made the work done by him as a volunteer the more specially noticeable. The strain and hardship brought on a sickness which necessitated his going to hospital for a short time during the siege, yet, in spite of this, he resumed his duty at the earliest chance.

Mr Russell's arduous, willing, and self-denying services in the commissariat, where he had charge of and dealt out daily the rations of the plainer foodstuff to foreigners and natives, excited general admiration, and they were always rendered with the greatest cheerfulness. The important and difficult work of milling the grain, in obtaining which he was also largely instrumental, was also entrusted to him.

I cannot conclude this despatch without saying a word of praise respecting the ladies of all nationalities who so ably and devotedly assisted the defence, notwithstanding the terrible shadow which at all times hung over the legation—a shadow which the never-ceasing rattle of musketry and crash of round shot and shell and the diminishing number of defenders rendered ever present. They behaved with infinite patience and cheerfulness, helping personally in the hospital or, in making sandbags and bandages, and in assisting in every possible way the work of defence. Especially commended are two young ladies—Miss Myers and Miss Daisy Brazier—who daily filtered the water for the hospital, in tropical heat, and carried it with bullets whistling and shells bursting in the trees overhead.

The Marquess of Lansdowne to Sir C. MacDonald

Sir,   *Foreign Office, February* 10, 1901

I have received and laid before the King your despatch of the 24th December, enclosing a report, in continuation of those already received, with accompanying maps, on events at Peking from the 20th June to the 14th August regarded from the military aspect.

As the present report completes your account of the siege and relief of the Legations, I desire to take this opportunity of stating how highly His Majesty's Government value these admirable and exhaustive records of an episode of the deepest historic interest.

The gallantry with which the defence was maintained by all the foreign forces engaged, more especially after the failure of the first relief expedition, and the consequent disappointment to the besieged, coupled with the energy and courage with which the efforts of the regular forces were seconded by the Legation staffs and other civilians, has commanded the admiration of the whole civilized world.

His Majesty's Government desire also to place on record their appreciation of the important part borne by yourself throughout this crisis. On the 22nd June, at the request of your colleagues, you took charge of the defence, a position for which, from your military training, you possessed exceptional qualifications; and from that date you continued to direct the operations of the garrison until the relief took place on the 14th August.

Information has reached His Majesty's Government from various sources that the success of the defence was largely due to your personal efforts, and more particularly to the unity and cohesion which you found means of establishing and maintaining among the forces of so many different nationalities operating over an extended area. Competent eye-witnesses have expressed the opinion that if it can be said that the European community owe their lives to any one man more than to another, where so many distinguished themselves, it is to you they are indebted for their safety.

I cannot conclude this despatch without asking you to convey to Lady MacDonald the thanks of His Majesty's Government for her unceasing and devoted attention to the comfort and welfare of the sick and wounded. Her work, and that of the ladies who assisted her, have earned the lasting gratitude not only of those who benefited by her ministrations, but also of their relatives in Europe who were kept for so many weeks in a condition of the most painful anxiety and suspense.

LANSDOWNE

Other titles in the series

The Amritsar Massacre: General Dyer in the Punjab, 1919

"We feel that General Dyer, by adopting an inhuman and un-British method of dealing with subjects of His Majesty the King-Emperor, has done great disservice to the interest of British rule in India. This aspect it was not possible for the people of the mentality of General Dyer to realise."

Backdrop

At the time of the events described, India was under British rule. Indians had fought alongside the British in World War I, and had made tremendous financial contributions to the British war effort. Mahatma Gandhi was the leader of the Indian National Congress party, which was seeking independence from the British Empire.

The Book

This is the story of the action taken by Brigadier-General Dyer at Amritsar in the Punjab in 1919. Faced with insurrection in support of Mahatma Gandhi, the British Army attempted to restore order. General Dyer, on arriving in the troubled city of Amritsar, issued an order banning any assembly of more than four people. Consequently, when he discovered a large crowd gathered together during a cattle fair, he took the astonishing action of shooting more than three hundred unarmed people. Regarding the subsequent native obedience as a satisfactory result, he was surprised to find himself removed from command a year later, and made lengthy representations to Parliament.

ISBN 0 11 702412 0   Price £6.99

British Battles of World War I, 1914–15

"The effect of these poisonous gases was so virulent as to render the whole of the line held by the French Division incapable of any action at all. It was at first impossible for anyone to realise what had actually happened. The smoke and fumes hid everything from sight, and hundreds of men were thrown into a comatose or dying condition, and within an hour the whole position had to be abandoned, together with about 50 guns."

Backdrop

On 4 August 1914, Britain declared war on Germany. Germany had already invaded Belgium and France and was progressing towards Paris.

The Book

These are the despatches from some of the battles of the first two years of World War I. They include action in northern France, Germany, Gallipoli, and even as far afield as the Cocos Islands in the Indian Ocean. They describe the events of battle, the tremendous courage, the huge losses, and the confusions and difficulties of war. These startling accounts, which were written by the generals at the front, were first published in the "London Gazette", the official newspaper of Parliament.

ISBN 0 11 702447 3   Price £6.99

Florence Nightingale and the Crimea, 1854–55

"By an oversight, no candles were included among the stores brought to the Crimea. Lamps and wicks were brought but not oil. These omissions were not supplied until after possession had been taken of Balaklava, and the purveyor had an opportunity of purchasing candles and oil from the shipping and the dealers in the town."

Backdrop

The British Army arrived in the Crimea in 1854, ill-equipped to fight a war in the depths of a Russian winter.

The Book

The hospital service for wounded soldiers during the Crimean War was very poor and became the subject of concern, not just in the army, but also in the press. "The Times" was publishing letters from the families of soldiers describing the appalling conditions. This embarrassed the government, but even more it irritated the army, which did not know how to cope with such open scrutiny of its activities.

The book is a collection of extracts from government papers published in 1855 and 1856. Their selection provides a snapshot of events at that time. In particular they focus on the terrible disaster that was the Charge of the Light Brigade, and the inadequate provisions that were made for the care of the sick and wounded. The documents relating to the hospitals at Scutari include evidence from Florence Nightingale herself.

ISBN 0 11 702425 2   Price £6.99

Lord Kitchener and Winston Churchill: The Dardanelles Commission Part I, 1914–15

"The naval attack on the Narrows was never resumed. It is difficult to understand why the War Council did not meet between 19th March and 14th May. The failure of the naval attack showed the necessity of abandoning the plan of forcing the passage of the Dardanelles by purely naval operation. The War Council should then have met and considered the future policy to be pursued."

Backdrop

The Dardanelles formed part of the main southern shipping route to Russia, and was of great military and strategic importance. However, it had long been recognised by the British naval and military authorities that any attack on the Dardanelles would be an operation fraught with great difficulties.

The Book

During the early stages of World War I, Russia made a plea to her allies to make a demonstration against the Turks. So attractive was the prize of the Dardanelles to the British generals, notably Lord Kitchener, that this ill-fated campaign was launched. Just how powerful an influence Kitchener was to exert over the War Council, and just how ill-prepared the Allies were to conduct such an attack, are revealed in dramatic detail in the report of this Commission.

The book covers the first part of the Commission's report. It deals with the origin, inception and conduct of operations in the Dardanelles from the beginning of the war in August 1914 until March 1915, when the idea of a purely naval attack was abandoned.

ISBN 0 11 702423 6   Price £6.99

The Russian Revolution, 1917

"It is the general opinion in Ekaterinburg that the Empress, her son, and four daughters were not murdered, but were despatched on the 17th July to the north or the west. The story that they were burnt in a house seems to be an exaggeration of the fact that in a wood outside the town was found a heap of ashes, apparently the result of burning a considerable amount of clothing. At the bottom of the ashes was a diamond, and, as one of the Grand Duchesses is said to have sewn a diamond into the lining of her cloak, it is supposed that the clothes of the Imperial family were burnt there."

Backdrop

By November 1917 Russia had lost more than twenty million people in the war. Lenin's Bolshevik party had overthrown the Tsar and had called for an end to all capitalist governments.

The Book

Government files contain a number of detailed documents describing the nature of the Bolshevik Revolution and the government of Lenin, which was observed to be not only abhorrent but also menacing because of the international implications. The book is compiled from two of these files, one of which describes the events leading up to the revolution and how the Bolsheviks came to power in October 1917. The other contains a series of eye-witness accounts of the frightening days of the Bolshevik regime from the summer of 1918 to April 1919.

ISBN 0 11 702424 4   Price £6.99

UFOs in the House of Lords, 1979

"Is it not time that Her Majesty's Government informed our people of what they know about UFOs? The UFOs have been coming in increasing numbers for 30 years since the war, and I think it is time our people were told the truth. We have not been invaded from outer space. Most incidents have not been hostile. Indeed it is us, the earthlings, who have fired on them. . . . Whatever the truth is, I am sure that an informed public is a prepared one. Another thing: it is on record that both sighting and landing reports are increasing all the time. Just suppose the 'ufonauts' decided to make mass landings tomorrow in this country—there could well be panic here, because our people have not been prepared."

Backdrop

The winter of 1978/79 in Britain was a time of strikes and unrest. It became known as the "winter of discontent". Yet it seems that the House of Lords had other more important things to discuss.

The Book

The book is the transcript of a debate in the House of Lords which took place in February 1979. Their Lordships debated the need for an international initiative in response to the problem of Unidentified Flying Objects. There were several notable speeches from noble lords and distinguished prelates.

ISBN 0 11 702413 9   Price £6.99

D Day to VE Day: General Eisenhower's Report, 1944–45

"During the spring of 1945, as the sky grew darker over Germany, the Nazi leaders had struggled desperately, by every means in their power, to whip their people into a last supreme effort to stave off defeat, hoping against hope that it would be possible, if only they could hold out long enough, to save the day by dividing the Allies. Blinded as they were by their own terror and hatred of 'Bolshevism', they were incapable of understanding the strength of the bond of common interest existing between Britain, the United States and the Soviet Union."

Backdrop

In 1944 the Allies were poised to launch an attack against Hitler's German war machine. The planning and timing were crucial. In February, General Eisenhower was appointed Supreme Commander of the Allied Operations in Europe.

The Book

The book is Dwight D. Eisenhower's personal account of the Allied invasion of Europe, from the preparations for the D-Day landings in Normandy, France, to the final assault across Germany. He presents a story of a far more arduous struggle than is commonly portrayed against an enemy whose tenacity he admired and whose skills he feared. It is a tactical account of his understanding of enemy manoeuvres, and his attempts to counter their actions. The formality of the report is coloured by many personal touches, and the reader senses Eisenhower's growing determination to complete the task. Hindsight would have had the general take more notice of Russian activity, but that this was not obvious to him is one of the fascinations of such a contemporary document.

ISBN 0 11 702451 1   Price £6.99